HIDDEN TRUTHS STRIPPED FROM

the

NATIONAL DIALOGUE

BEAUFORT
BOOKS

FIRST EDITION

Library of Congress Cataloging-in-Publication Data available upon request

For inquiries about volume orders, please contact:
Beaufort Books
27 West 20th Street, Suite 1102
New York, NY 10011
sales@beaufortbooks.com

Published in the United States by Beaufort Books
www.beaufortbooks.com

Distributed by Midpoint Trade Books
www.midpointtrade.com

ISBN: 9780825308321

Printed in the United States of America

HIDDEN TRUTHS STRIPPED FROM

the

NATIONAL DIALOGUE

A Reference For Those

Who Pursue a Role

In U.S. Leadership

Expiration Date: Best If Read Prior To 21st Birthday

BRUCE HERSCHENSOHN

AUTHOR'S NOTES

Details can be skipped if the reader prefers. Those details can easily be identified as they are enclosed in brackets: [ ]. The size of each chapter is not for any particular length but for the covering of the immediate subject of the chapter. Some portions of subjects are adapted from previous writings or forums of mine largely brought up to date.

The writing of this book was completed on December the 14th, 2015.

INTRODUCTION

Don't blame all those in the preceding generation or generations for telling you false information. How could they all have known the truth if they were never told the truth? They might well have been victims rather than conspirators. More precisely, it is likely that some who gave you inaccurate information were never allowed to see the face of truth before the masks had been tightly fastened over the passing history by many in major academia and major media.

Imagine that today you are liberal but every professor you have and every television network news of the day has a conservative bias all with the same conservative opinion as the other. No liberal view anywhere on TV. Imagine as well that every news magazine and newspaper has a conservative Republican view. Now, in reverse, imagine you are conservative but every television network news has identical liberal opinions and every news magazine and newspaper has a liberal Democrat opinion as well.

In truth, that liberal view was represented throughout most of the 1960s, all of the 1970s, 1980s, most of the 1990s and not exclusively but a majority of television networks into the current of the 21st Century. During most of the pre-cable years there were only three major television networks: ABC, CBS, and NBC. All three had the same political identity: liberal. The major news magazines were *Time* and *Newsweek*: both liberal. The major newspapers of the nation with syndicates whose reports were published in hundreds of newspapers throughout the nation were liberal and those newspapers with big syndicates were *The New York Times*, the *Washington Post*, and the *Los Angeles Times*. Compounding all this is that the unelected government bureaucracy widely held the same political philosophy of the major media and academia. Unless you were a subscriber to the *National Review* magazine of Bill Buckley you probably didn't get any information through the prism of a different political view.

This is not merely some remote unimportant history; instead it is likely the reason so many believe things about the times before their birth or prior to their memories that are not true. It is most doubtful that so many parents or grandparents have lied. It is that most likely they didn't know the truth. It is because what they saw, heard and read about what was going on in the world was consistently told by those with one view. It is likely many people of all ages now believe these myths since they have travelled with the generations. People in the current generation have come to believe conclusions from those older who heard second-hand and more than second-hand; third or fourth-hand during decades now gone.

CHAPTER ONE

MOST OFTEN REPORTED AND TAUGHT: (2011 FORWARD) "AFGHANISTAN IS THE LONGEST WAR IN THE USA's HISTORY"

THE TRUTH: NOT EVEN CLOSE

It became a repeated theme as the U.S. war in Afghanistan was heading toward its tenth anniversary. By the date of that tenth anniversary, October the 7th, 2011; the theme of an inaccurate role for Afghanistan as being our longest war had become repeated and repeated publically by the Obama Administration and its supporters.

In truth, the Cold War was our longest war lasting 46 years. Just one theater of that war, Vietnam, lasted 17 years.

Even when President Obama said he ended the combat mission in Afghanistan on December the 28th of 2014, he put into that statement: "...Our combat mission in Afghanistan is ending and the longest war in American history is coming to a responsible conclusion."

Wrong on all counts.

Under the Obama Administration the State Department was directed to encourage calculations of Afghanistan being the longest war of the U.S., and to help do that, when asked, skip the Eisenhower and Kennedy Administrations in Vietnam, helping to clear the way for Afghanistan to even walk over that single theater of the Cold War. That would help fuel the way for the withdrawal from Afghanistan. The Department of Defense didn't go along with such an absurd scheme while the State Department was enjoying itself.

No one from the media who attended the State Department's Press Briefings asked why there was a new invisibility of the Eisenhower and Kennedy Administrations. But with so many Vietnam Veterans still living as well as other U.S. Veterans who fought in other theaters of the Cold War there was a clear frustration in listening to the phrase of contradiction. President Obama's statement regarding what he said was the longest war in the history of the United States had the effect that the withdrawal from there was needed because Afghanistan was too long an involvement, inconsistent with the past involvements of the U.S.

Premature withdrawal, however, proved to be an invitation to the Taliban to attempt a comeback to power. [The Taliban had been the government in Afghanistan, hosting al-Qaeda as it prepared and launched the attacks of 9-11, 2001, on the United States and before the U.S. had launched Operation Enduring Freedom on October the 7th of 2001 which was 26 days after 9-11. The Taliban gave up its leadership of the Afghanistan government 39 days after the beginning of Operation Enduring Freedom.] But that history is too often lost in the easier memory of the phrase that had now been said so often that Afghanistan is "the longest war in U.S. history."

All of this proves that if the people are told the same thing enough times, most come to believe it. The avoided simplicity was that all that needed to be done was for anyone to count as far as 46 for the Cold War and as far as 17 for U.S. involvement in the Vietnam Theater of that war. The mystery is why so many brilliant people apparently couldn't count—or that so many of the ones who could count would not bother to do it.

CHAPTER TWO

MOST OFTEN REPORTED AND TAUGHT: (1978, 1995-96, 2013, 2014, 2015) "THE FEDERAL GOVERNMENT COULD BE SHUT DOWN AGAIN"

THE TRUTH:

IT WAS NEVER SHUT DOWN, AND THE U.S. GOVERNMENT REMAINS MOST UNLIKELY TO EVER BE SHUT DOWN

It was an unlikely question while President Obama met with President Xi Jinping of the People's Republic of China [September 25, 2015]: A member of the press-corps asked President Obama if he would be able to work with the Congress "at a time when you're trying to negotiate to avert a government shutdown."

Explaining why he felt a government shutdown would be terrible, President Obama said: "Hopefully they've (Congress) learned some lessons from 2011, the last time they sought to introduce (a) non-budget item into the budget discussions. At that (time), it was Obama Care, and they were going to shut down the government for that purpose." He went on to suggest what could be lost in such a government lockout: "Our military provides us protection; our agencies keep our air clean and our water clean. And our people every single day are helping to respond to emergencies, and helping families get Social Security checks, and helping them deal with an ailing parent. And when you insist that 'unless I get my way on this one particular issue I'm going to shut down all those services'—and by the way, leave a whole lot of really hardworking people without paychecks—that doesn't just hurt the economy; that hurts—in the abstract—it hurts particular families. And as I recall, it wasn't particularly good for the reputation of the Republican Party either."

He either did not know what a government shutdown means or he didn't want the people of the country to know. What has generally been called "closing down the government" has been a close-down of only those parts of government that are non-essential. The military stays intact as defense does not close. Social Security checks continue to go out to recipients. The Postal Service remains open as does the Border Patrol and Federal Prisons and the power grid and the Veteran's Administration and on and on the list goes including the Affordable Care Act (popularly known as Obama-Care) and unemployment benefits and food stamps and many, many other government operations.

If there is a threat of a close-down, about 800,000 non-essential government workers will have to stay home without scheduled pay. That still leaves 1,300,000 federal civilian employees at work plus, of course, 1,400,000 members of the military and 500,000 postal employees. They are all essential and all essential elements of government remain in operation.

If past such "close-downs" will be repeated, recognize that in most cases it wasn't that non-essentials were unpaid; it was that they were paid retroactively when the budget was back in business. For many it was terribly difficult and for others it was a paid vacation with the pay coming late. There, too, were other inconveniences; particularly the closing of National Parks and the decision of President Obama to stop tours through the White House.

When it came to the 2014 dispute on using fear to suggest that the Department of Homeland Security would close down, out of the 230,000 employees there, 210,000 would still be working while 20,000 would not because they were non-essential.

It should be considered that what is called "a close-down of government" be made permanent. That way, only the essential operations would remain filled without taxpayer's money collected for non-essential operations. This should be considered essential in itself, as our national debt has increased above eighteen trillion dollars. What are we doing paying the 800,000 non-essential employees?

CHAPTER THREE

MOST OFTEN REPORTED AND TAUGHT:
(Many Years)
"BOTH THE PRESIDENT AND THE CONGRESS HAVE EQUAL JURISDICTIONS OVER DOMESTIC AND FOREIGN POLICIES"

THE TRUTH:
PRESIDENTIAL AND CONGRESSIONAL AREAS OF JURISDICTION DO NOT HAVE EQUAL AUTHORITIES

There was a message from President Kennedy waiting for Former Vice President Nixon. To the public they had been rivals in the Presidential election of 1960. To those who knew them, the rivalry was temporary while their friendship was permanent. On this day, [April 20, 1961,] three months after the Inauguration of President Kennedy and three days after the failed invasion of the Bay of Pigs in Cuba, the new President asked Richard Nixon, the former Vice President of President Eisenhower to meet with him at the White House.

He did.

President Kennedy was totally involved at the horror of what had happened at the Bay of Pigs in Cuba. He was wrapped in a mixture of frustration, anger, and most of all sadness at the lives lost there. Despite all that overpowering emotion he was considerate enough to move from his desk as it was likely the first time that Former Vice President Nixon was in that office after seeing President Eisenhower sit behind that desk for the past eight years. President Kennedy moved to his rocking chair across from where the Former Vice President who was already positioned where President Kennedy had indicated for him to sit on a heavily cushioned lounge chair.

As they faced each other without any barriers of furniture, the discussion changed to what President Kennedy should do now regarding Fidel Castro still "ninety miles away from our shores" and then the subject was changed again, this time from the recent and possible future events in Cuba to a "conversational tour around the world" to the many places of conflict in which the United States, and therefore President Kennedy, would have to be deeply engaged. As they started that part of the conversation President Kennedy rose from his rocking chair and he started pacing. The subjects were Cuba, West Berlin, Laos, South Vietnam, the Congo, India versus Pakistan, Indonesia versus the U.N., and the leaders of all of them, especially Mao Tse-tung of the People's Republic of China and most of all, Nikita Khrushchev of the Soviet Union.

According to both President Nixon and Pierre Salinger, President Kennedy's Press Secretary and close friend, that was when the President stopped his pacing and with a slight smile stared at the eyes of the Former Vice President and then made a statement that was cloaked as a question: "This is the stuff of Presidents, isn't it?"

Former Vice President Nixon nodded slowly. "It is, Mister President."

President Kennedy then gave statements about the Presidential authority over foreign affairs and, in contrast, how the Congress is needed for determination of most domestic and economic issues. He gave as illustration the then-current debate over whether or not the minimum wage should be raised one dime an hour from $1.15 to $1.25. President Kennedy stated the issue and then again turned a statement into a question: "I mean who cares if the minimum wage is $1.15 or $1.25?"

Again, the Former Vice President nodded, this time adding his own smile.

Neither of them really meant they didn't care about the minimum wage; of course they cared, but the determination would be up to the Congress, not the President. On the other hand, it is the President, not the Congress, who has final determination over foreign affairs. President Kennedy was at this time taking the public's blame for the failure of the conclusion of the Bay of Pigs invasion—and in the year to come he would justifiably be given the credit for the success of the Cuban Missile Crisis. It was, in fact, "The Stuff of Presidents" as the Congress had not known about either of those policies in advance: the Bay of Pigs, or what he would do about Soviet missiles in Cuba.

President Kennedy knew he had more authority to retain or raise the minimum wage when he was a Congressman or a Senator than he did as President. All he could do as President was advocate and try to influence his position to the Congress, but not appropriate funds. Although he was able to convince the Congress on that one, he was unable to win on legislation regarding a number of wider policy advocacies, failing to convince the Congress to pass his major tax reductions and civil rights legislation, neither of which he was able to get passed through the Congress while he was President. [It wasn't until after his assassination in 1963, that both presidential pursuits passed as 1964 Acts of the Congress and signed by President Lyndon Baines Johnson.]

Seven Presidents after President Kennedy, President Clinton couldn't get his health care plan through the Congress. But when he wanted the U.S. military to intervene in Bosnia against Milosevic's Serbia, and when he wanted a four-day bombing raid on Saddam Hussein's Iraq so as to get rid of Iraq's weapons of mass destruction, and when he intervened in Kosovo against Milosevic of Serbia's "ethnic cleansing", and when he wanted to send the U.S. Navy to Haiti to establish Operation Uphold Democracy, he took those military actions.

President George W. Bush (43) couldn't get Congress to pass his Social Security Reform or Immigration Reform. But when he wanted the U.S. military to go into Afghanistan and when he wanted the U.S. military to go into Iraq, he took those military actions.

When President Obama followed him into office, the new President wanted his own health-care plan put into law. His comfortable majority in the 111th Congress eventually voted for it but it took him a year to get it through passage of the Congress and without his single-payer system that he wanted. But when President Obama gave timelines for the U.S. military to leave Iraq and Afghanistan, he just ordered the timelines. And when he wanted the U.S. military to intervene in Libya and then put NATO rather than the United States in charge of the action, he did it.

For sure, the Congress has influence with the President and the President has influence with the Congress and both have influence with the public, but when it comes to resolution of policies, with the exception of a sustained veto of the President, the Congress generally has the final word on domestic matters, and with little exception foreign policy decisions are, as President Kennedy called them,

"The Stuff of Presidents." Or as President George W. Bush was to say [during a controversy with the press as he voiced confidence in his Secretary of Defense against critics] "Mine is the final decision... I'm the decider." The President's foreign policies remain intact.

[Presidents must seek the Senate's advice and consent for Treaties but often Presidents avoid that by making Executive Agreements or Accords or Communiqués with foreign governments rather than Treaties. Also in the field of foreign affairs, Presidents must seek the Senate's advice and consent for appointments of U.S. Ambassadors and other officers administering foreign policy departments, agencies, and bureaus of government.]

Historically, disregarding personal issues or scandals or assassination, the events that most instantly come to mind regarding Presidents since the United States became the world's leading international power, are generally issues of foreign policy, overtaking domestic issues: Truman with the Atom Bomb; Eisenhower with the cease-fire in Korea; Kennedy with the Cuban Missile Crisis; Johnson with Vietnam; Nixon with Vietnam and opening the door to China; (Ford for no particular policy either foreign or domestic;) Carter with the Iranian Hostage Crisis; Reagan with "Mr. Gorbachev, Tear Down This Wall!"; Bush (41) with the Liberation of Kuwait; (Clinton for no particular policy either foreign or domestic having come into office after the Cold War was won and before 9-11 occurred); and Bush (43) with the military interventions in Afghanistan and Iraq. (At this writing Obama's Presidency has yet to be completed.)

Constitutional procedure dictates that in most domestic affairs, even when a President opposes some bill that originates in the Congress, the Congress can pass the bill. The President, of course, can refuse to sign it—vetoing the bill, but the Congress can override the President's veto and the President is out of constitutional means as he cannot veto their override. The Congress, therefore, generally has the domestic policy role of "decider."

Nothing proved the point of congressional preeminence in domestic affairs overriding the President as convincingly as President Obama's speech to a Joint Session of the Congress on September the 8th of 2011 when he literally begged the members of the Congress to pass his "American Jobs" bill. If nothing else, his repeated appeal within that speech was a public admission that the Congress was needed for its passage. Some excerpts of the speech in the order in which they occurred were: "I am sending this Congress a plan that you should pass right away...You should pass this jobs plan right away...Pass this jobs bill—pass this jobs bill...Pass this jobs bill...You should pass it right away...You should pass it right away...Pass this jobs bill...Pass this bill...Pass this jobs bill...Pass this bill...Pass this jobs bill...Pass this jobs bill...Pass this bill right away...Regardless of the arguments we've had in the past, regardless of the arguments we'll have in the future, this plan is the right thing to do right now. You should pass it." They passed parts of it. Even those parts took the Congress nearly seven months. [April the 5th of 2012.]

In the most recent (at this writing) series of debates by presidential aspirants facing state caucuses and primaries, by far the most questions asked were concerning issues over which those answering would not have control should they become president. Most questions and subsequent answers were, in fact, a waste of time, and worse than a waste of time, created an impression to voters that a president would have the power to do all things discussed in those debates. This was not unique to that presidential election period, but normal for most presidential elections.

Out of it all, since they heard themselves in their own campaigns, elected presidents often come into office with grand plans for domestic affairs, having given too little emphasis to foreign policy in their campaigns.

If people knew that simple truth of final authorities, they would think differently before supporting or opposing a Congressional candidate and differently before supporting or opposing a Presidential candidate. But most voters don't know who has final authority over what. Worst of all, some elected presidents start a presidency aiming at the wrong policy targets. Even though much of their earlier time in office is wasted on such issues, most presidents eventually catch on.

They have to catch on since after all, the stuff of Presidents is foreign affairs because the United States cannot have 535 Commanders in Chief. Just one.

CHAPTER FOUR

MOST OFTEN REPORTED AND TAUGHT: (1964 Forward) "IF PRESIDENT KENNEDY HAD LIVED HE WOULD HAVE WITHDRAWN THE UNITED STATES FROM VIETNAM"

THE TRUTH: IN HIS OWN WORDS

Less than three months before President Kennedy was assassinated, he appeared on the new television half-hour CBS Evening News with his segment having been video-taped at Hyannis Port on the morning of September the 2nd, 1963. The conversation turned to Vietnam:

President Kennedy: "I don't agree with those who say we should withdraw. That would be a great mistake. I know people don't like Americans to be engaged in this kind of effort. Forty-seven Americans have been killed in combat with the enemy. But this is a very important struggle even though it is far away. We took all this—made this effort to defend Europe. Now Europe is quite secure. We also have to participate—we may not like it—in the defense of Asia."

One week later, on September the 9th of 1963, President Kennedy appeared on NBC's "Huntley-Brinkley Report." To David Brinkley he said, "We can't make the world over, but we can influence the world. The fact of the matter is that with the assistance of the United States, SEATO, Southeast Asia and indeed all of Asia has been maintained independent against a powerful force, the Chinese Communists. What I am concerned about is that Americans will get impatient and say because they don't like events in Southeast Asia or they don't like the government in Saigon, that we should withdraw. That only makes it easy for the Communists. I think we should stay. We should use our influence in as effective a way as we can, but we should not withdraw."

Three days later, on September the 12th of 1963, President Kennedy held a News Conference in the State Department Auditorium in which he said: "I think I have stated what my view is and we are for those things and those policies which help win the war there. That is why some 25,000 Americans have traveled 10,000 miles to participate in that struggle. What helps to win the war, we support; what interferes with the war effort, we oppose. I have already made it clear that any action by either government which may handicap the winning of the war is inconsistent with our policy or our objectives...

"In some ways I think the Vietnamese people and ourselves agree; we want the war to be won, the Communists to be contained, and the Americans to go home. That is our policy. I am sure it is the policy of the people of Vietnam. But we are not there to see a war lost, and we will follow the policy which I have indicated today of advancing those causes and issues which help win the war."

It was two months and ten days later, on November the 22nd of 1963 that President Kennedy was assassinated. He had planned to deliver two speeches on that day: one at the Trade Mart in Dallas that afternoon, and one in the evening at the Municipal Auditorium in Austin. Both of the speeches were to have emphasized the build-up made in the nation's defenses. In Dallas he planned on recognizing the major nations to whom our military assistance was given: "Vietnam, Free China [not the PRC but Free China in reference to the people on Taiwan], [S.] Korea, India, Pakistan, Thailand, Greece, Turkey, and Iran [the Shah's government, some 15 years prior to the Radical Islamist Revolution]." And he planned on having said, "Our assistance to these nations can be painful, risky and costly, as is true in Southeast Asia today. But we dare not weary of the task."

In Austin he was going to recall a pledge he made in 1960 to "build a national defense in which is not 'first but,' not 'first if,' not 'first when,' but 'first—period.' The pledge has been fulfilled."

It was.

The great majority of the United States had been on the side of former President Eisenhower's policy and President Kennedy's policy continuing the defense of South Vietnam. If President Kennedy wanted to change the U.S. policy on Vietnam from the U.S. military involvement helping South Vietnam from North Vietnam's continuing invasion of troops and attacks, he certainly would have wanted to influence the U.S. public to endorse any planned withdrawal. In a democracy, public approval of presidential policy is always a pursuit of the President. There was no question he was attempting to influence most Americans to continue to endorse his policy toward Vietnam rather than withdrawal. But after the assassination of the

President, many started the word that President Kennedy would have withdrawn from Vietnam had he lived. They were, in fact, as inaccurate as those who later didn't even count his presidential years as being involved in Vietnam. Most likely it was that after his assassination it was their cause to withdraw but it had not been the President's cause. They apparently forgot his own words.

CHAPTER FIVE

MOST OFTEN REPORTED AND TAUGHT: (1964-1975) "MAKE LOVE, NOT WAR!"

THE TRUTH:

THAT WAS HOW THE 94th U.S. CONGRESS ACHIEVED U.S. AND SOUTH VIETNAMESE DEFEAT SNATCHED FROM THE VICTORY OF THE UNITED STATES AND SOUTH VIETNAMESE ARMED FORCES

At the White House January the 23rd of 1973 was called V-V Day in the same and appropriate designation that had been used 27 years earlier on May the 8th of 1945 when V-E Day was used to refer to Victory in Europe and September the 2nd of 1945 when V-J Day was used to refer to Victory over Japan. The U.S. Department of Defense also regarded this day in 1973 as V-V Day, but the Department of State didn't and many entertainment celebrities didn't and the majority of the 93rd Congress didn't. That was particularly true since so many State Department careerists didn't want the victory of the U.S. and South Vietnam, and so many entertainment figures and members of the 93rd Congress made a semi-career of participating in Anti-U.S. Policy Demonstrations and they had made speeches with the themes that "We should never have gotten into Vietnam; the South Vietnamese are running away from battles; the U.S. military is losing; and it's time to pack up and 'Come Home, America!' and 'Stop the Killing!' And 'Make Love, Not War!'"

One month earlier President Nixon had asked a number of those on his staff if they thought there should be a U.S. bombing pause for Christmas. He made it clear he favored such a pause for Christmas, but wanted their opinions. One of the responses to his request was "Don't stop the bombing. The enemy will use any pause to increase their arms, regroup and realign themselves on the Ho Chi Minh Trail and we'll pay the price. Besides, North Vietnam is an atheist-governed country that doesn't celebrate Christmas—not that the government there concerns itself with anyone's holiday. They used the truce of Tet—the Lunar New Year's Day in 1968—for their offensive against South Vietnam. I don't believe they should be trusted to take a Christmas holiday from their war."

The President overrode that opinion and followed his own instincts by calling for a 36 hour bombing pause for Christmas. [Six hours on Christmas Eve, twenty-four hours on Christmas, and six hours on the 26th.] That was of no consequence to many journalists, historians, and academics who referred to it (with many still referring to it) as "The Christmas Bombing," a phrase of religious insensitivity.

The bombing had started on December 18, 1972 and after that intermission of 36 hours over Christmas, the bombing was resumed and then ended on December 29 after the North Vietnamese agreed to come back to the peace talks in Paris if we wouldn't restart the bombing. The President had also planned a 36 hour bombing pause for the New Year's Day holiday but U.S. bombing had already stopped two days prior to the New Year. The Paris talks restarted on January 8, 1973. Before the month was done North Vietnam's signature was on the document of agreement.

Five weeks after the signing, an act of confirmation was signed [on March the 2nd] by the representatives of eleven nations plus the Viet Cong in the Act of the International Conference of Vietnam. [The eleven nations were Canada, France, Hungary, Indonesia, North Vietnam, People's Republic of China, Poland, United Kingdom, Union of Soviet Socialist Republics, United States of America, and South Vietnam.] The Act called for "respect of the Vietnamese people's fundamental national rights, and the South Vietnamese people's right to self determination...The Parties to this Act solemnly acknowledge the commitments by the parties to the Agreement and the Protocols to strictly respect and scrupulously implement the Agreement and the Protocols" and in the event of a violation, "the parties signatory to the Agreement and the Protocols shall, either individually or jointly, consult with the other Parties to this Act with a view to determining necessary remedial measures."

Most significantly, the Act was signed by Andrei Gromyko, the Minister of Foreign Affairs for the government of the Union of Soviet Socialist Republics, and Chi Peng-Fei, the Minister of Foreign Affairs for the government of the People's Republic of China.

In the 40 days between the beginning of the bombing that brought about the Peace Accords, and the signing of the Paris Peace Accords, the American people had been told the following from prominent names in the U.S. media:

A *Washington Post* editorial commented that President Nixon conducted a bombing policy "so ruthless and so difficult to fathom politically, as to cause millions of Americans to cringe in shame and to wonder at their President's very sanity."

Joseph Kraft, a leading journalist whose syndicated columns appeared in newspapers throughout the nation, wrote: "Mr. Nixon called on the bombers—an action, in my judgment, of senseless terror which stains the good name of America."

Journalist James Reston, who was the Vice President of *The New York Times* wrote: "This is war by tantrum."

Anthony Lewis (*The New York Times)* wrote, "Even with sympathy for the men who fly American planes, and for their families, one has to recognize the greater courage of the North Vietnamese people...The elected leader of the greatest democracy acts like a maddened tyrant...To send B52's against populous areas such as Hanoi or Haiphong can have only one purpose: terror. It was the response of a man so overwhelmed by his sense of inadequacy and frustration that he had to strike out, punish, destroy."

The New York Times reported that waves of bombers "flying in wedges of three, lay down more than 65 tons of bombs at a time, in a carpet pattern one and one-half miles long and one mile wide ...the most intensive aerial bombardment in history...equivalent to twenty of the atomic bombs dropped on Hiroshima." *The Times* informed its readers that all of this was occurring in "densely populated areas." [Hanoi's own figures, released at the time, put the total number of civilian casualties during the 12-day campaign at 1,300-1,600, far below the estimates of casualties in Hiroshima. Now, as in World War II we were in a war we wanted to win.] Four months later, after American military involvement in Vietnam was over, *The New York Times* admitted that "Hanoi Films Show No Carpet Bombing." Although it was late, the earlier error was corrected.

Dan Rather (CBS) told his audience that the United States "has embarked on a large-scale terror bombing" with the operative word "unrestricted." He quoted Hanoi to the effect that the strikes were "extermination raids on many populous areas."

Harry Reasoner (ABC) told his audience that "Dr. Kissinger's boss had broken Dr. Kissinger's word. It's very hard to swallow."

Walter Cronkite (CBS) told his audience that the "Soviet News Agency Tass said hundreds of U.S. bombers destroyed thousands of homes, most of them in the Hanoi-Haiphong area...Hanoi Radio said the bombings indicate President Nixon has taken leave of his senses." He let the quote stand.

Eric Sevareid (CBS) told his audience, "In most areas of the government...the feeling is one of dismay, tinged with shame that the United States is again resorting to mass killing in an effort to end the killing."

The major media had been unbalanced for some time and they continued that imbalance: A study of the Institute for American Strategy concluded that during 1972 and 1973, CBS News balance between favorable and unfavorable stories regarding U.S. military affairs was: 13% favorable, 66.1% unfavorable. The study found that in 1972 some 83.33% of themes in CBS stories about South Vietnam were critical of the Saigon government, while 57.32% about North Vietnam were favorable to the Hanoi government. Within the same year the study found that CBS quoted the statements of those who were critical of our policy 842 times, while those in favor of our policy were quoted 23 times.

Prominent among television specials on the war had been the CBS presentation of a travelogue of North Vietnam narrated by John Hart of CBS, who reported from Hanoi:

"There is frequent laughter...Yesterday when I suggested that we'd like to get up early some morning to film the sunrise over one of these lakes, it was suggested that's a wonderful idea because after all, the American flyers cannot bomb the sun...Within a few hours of my arrival I have seen a richness in hospitality and a richness in hope...Five-thirty Sunday morning in Hanoi: This is the second Mass of the day. The cathedral is filled...American peace workers will be taken to see destroyed buildings and towns, and especially a number of destroyed or partially destroyed churches...There is a display of forgiveness by the villagers [toward captured pilots] ...being released under the humanitarian policy of the government."

As Americans watched his films, a painting was shown and the painting was described as "recalling a bay...lovely...before it was heavily bombed." There were films of hospitals and churches allegedly bombed and damaged by Americans. There were no films of factories or bridges or railroads or supply centers bombed. No bombed war objectives of any sort were shown.

John Hart of CBS continued the travelogue with interviews of captured American prisoners of war, and through John Hart and through CBS their statements went into the homes of Americans, just as Hanoi wanted: "'I have been well treated since my capture and I would like to thank the people for their kindness...their humanity has also been shown by their release of three prisoners recently...I hope my government may soon bring this war to an end...To my family, my lovely wife, I would wish that they select the candidate they feel will stop this war.'"

The North Vietnamese thought of their signing of the Paris Peace Accords as the day of its surrender under U.S. and South Vietnamese power as the U.S. military and the South Vietnamese military had won decisively by every conceivable measure. That was the accurate view of our enemy, the North Vietnamese Government Officials.

In summary, victory was apparent when President Nixon ordered the U.S. Air Force to bomb industrial and military targets in Hanoi, North Vietnam's capital city, and Haiphong, its major port city, and we would stop the bombing if the North Vietnamese would attend the Paris Peace Talks that they had left earlier having been on and off since the Johnson Administration and, beyond debate, it was the December, 1972 bombing of Hanoi and Haiphong that brought them back to the table. We then stopped the bombing as promised which was followed by the January 23rd, 1973, speech to the nation by President Nixon on primetime television announcing that the Paris Peace Accords had been initialed by the U.S., South Vietnam, North Vietnam, the Viet Cong, and the Accords would be signed on the 27th.

What the United States and South Vietnam achieved in those accords was North Vietnam's agreement that South Vietnam would retain its own government and we plagiarized our own First Amendment and added some freedoms for them in addition to the ones guaranteed in our own Constitution. On that issue, the Paris Peace Accords read: "Immediately after the cease-fire, the two South Vietnamese parties [The South Vietnam Government and the North Vietnam proxy: the Viet Cong] will: Achieve national reconciliation and concord, end hatred and enmity, prohibit all acts of reprisal and discrimination against individuals or organizations that have collaborated with one side or the other, insure the democratic liberties of the people: personal freedom, freedom of speech, freedom of the press, freedom of meeting, freedom of organization, freedom of political activities, freedom of belief, freedom of movement, freedom of residence, freedom of work, right to property ownership and right to free enterprise." [Chapter Four, Article Eleven]

Recognizing the habit of the North Vietnamese Government

officials breaking their word, the United States backed up its victory with a pledge: Should the South require any military hardware to defend itself against any North Vietnam aggression we would provide replacement aid to the South on a piece-by piece, one-to-one replacement meaning a gun for a gun; a bullet for a bullet; a helicopter for a helicopter, for all things lost—a replacement. The Soviet Union could also do it for their side (except, of course, South Vietnam had never attempted a takeover of North Vietnam. The entire conflict was over North Vietnam's invasion of the South so South Vietnam aggression was not a factor.) The piece-for-piece replacement [in Chapter Four, Article Seven] read: "The two South Vietnam parties [South Vietnam and the Viet Cong] shall be permitted to make periodic replacement of armaments, munitions and war material which have been destroyed, damaged, worn out or used up after the cease-fire, on the basis of piece-for-piece."

National Security Advisor Henry Kissinger explained, "There is a flat prohibition against the introduction of any military force into South Vietnam from outside of South Vietnam, which is to say that whatever forces may be in South Vietnam from outside South Vietnam, specifically North Vietnamese forces, cannot receive reinforcements, replacements or any other form of augmentation by any means whatsoever. With respect to military equipment, both sides are permitted to replace all existing military equipment on a one-to-one basis under international supervision and control."

The advance of communist tyranny had been halted by those accords.

And then it all came apart.

It happened this way: In August of the following year, 1974,

President Nixon resigned his office as a result of what became known as "Watergate." Three months after his resignation came the November congressional elections and within them the Democrats won a landslide victory for the new Congress that would convene in January of 1975.

It was the 94th Congress and many of the members used their new majority to defund the military aid the U.S. had promised, breaking the commitment we made to the South Vietnamese in Paris to provide whatever piece-for-piece military hardware the South Vietnamese needed in case of aggression from the North. Put simply and accurately, a majority of Democrats of the 94th Congress did not keep the word of the United States, and the members knew it.

Dr. Kissinger said that if he had any inkling that U.S. aid to American allies would be cut back, "I could not in good conscience have negotiated" the Paris Peace Accords.

The North Vietnamese leaders admitted they were testing the new President, Gerald Ford, and they took one village after another, then cities, then provinces and each escalating step was met by President Ford doing nothing until his April the 10th of 1975 speech when President Gerald Ford appealed directly to those members of the 94th Congress in an evening Joint Session of the Congress televised to the nation, in which he literally begged the Congress to keep the word of the United States.

But as President Ford delivered his speech, many of the members of the Congress walked out of the chamber. Many had an investment in America's failure in Vietnam. They had participated in demonstrations against U.S. policy for years.

They simply wouldn't give the aid and the President did not make the decision on his own even though he was constitutionally entitled to make that decision. Only one week after his speech on April the 17th Cambodia surrendered and the genocide there began. On April the 30th South Vietnam surrendered and Re-education Camps were constructed and the phenomenon of the Boat People began.

If the South Vietnamese had received the arms the United States promised them would the result have been different? It already had been different. But things drastically had changed: Bui Tin, the Colonel who demanded and received the surrender of Saigon said, "When Nixon stepped down because of Watergate we knew we would win." Pham Van Dong, the Prime Minister of North Vietnam said, "When Ford kept American B-52s in their hangers, our leadership decided on a big offensive against South Vietnam."

The U.S. did not resupply the South Vietnamese as we had promised even after the April 10th speech of President Ford and the North Vietnamese knew they were on the road to South Vietnam's capital city, Saigon, that would soon be renamed as Ho Chi Minh City.

The South Vietnamese had fought to the end of their ammunition.

Former Arkansas Senator William Fulbright, who had been the Chairman of the Senate Foreign Relations Committee made a public statement about the surrender of South Vietnam saying, "I am no more distressed than I would be about Arkansas losing a football game to Texas."

It took two and one-quarter years from achieving victory in Vietnam until the majority of the U.S. Congress succeeded in their quest to attain defeat.

Although the U.S. knew North Vietnam would violate the accords and although the U.S. and South Vietnam planned for it by the piece-replaced for any and every piece-lost, what the people of the United States did not even guess was that the U.S. Congress would violate the accords. And violate them, of all things, on behalf of the North Vietnamese. That is what happened.

CHAPTER SIX

MOST OFTEN REPORTED AND TAUGHT: (1997 Forward) "IN 1997 HONG KONG HAD TO BE GIVEN BACK TO THE PEOPLE'S REPUBLIC OF CHINA BECAUSE OF THE LEASE SIGNED BY GREAT BRITAIN IN 1898 FOR THE RETURN OF HONG KONG TO CHINA IN 99 YEARS"

THE TRUTH:

THAT 99 YEAR LEASE DID NOT COVER THE ISLAND OF HONG KONG NOR DID IT COVER THE KOWLOON PENINSULA, BOTH OF WHICH WERE GIVEN BY TREATIES TO GREAT BRITAIN IN PERPETUITY

The Treaty of Nanking was signed in 1842, giving the island of Hong Kong to Great Britain from the Emperor of China for Great Britain to have in perpetuity; forever.

The Treaty of Peking was signed in 1860 giving the Kowloon

Peninsula across from the island of Hong Kong to Great Britain from the Emperor of China for Great Britain to have in perpetuity; forever.

A lease of the New Territories north of the Kowloon Peninsula and south of China, was leased to Great Britain by China with the lease to be held by Great Britain for 99 years from 1898 to expiration in 1997.

As the years went on, those three entities; Hong Kong Island, Kowloon, and the New Territories became internationally known as one political entity called Hong Kong. If nothing else, brevity and simplicity indicated it, as all three were under Great Britain's jurisdiction with only the third entity on lease.

It was 1840 when Queen Victoria's Foreign Secretary of Great Britain Lord Palmerston called Hong Kong "a barren island with hardly a house upon it." He wanted an island like Hainan, not Hong Kong with a population of what British journalists said was 5,650 fishermen at best and for sure it was a pirate's hang-out. No matter; on January the 26th of 1841 the Union Jack was unfurled on what became "Possession Point of Hong Kong."

Advance the calendar to World War II when the Japanese Empire attacked Hong Kong simultaneous with its attack on Pearl Harbor, the Philippines, and Malaysia including Singapore. The Japanese military invaded the British territory from the Chinese border into the New Territories and worked their way southward. Prime Minister Winston Churchill gave the order for the British in Hong Kong to hold on. It was an impossible task but the fight went on for eighteen days and nights through the New Territories, through Kowloon and finally through Hong Kong Island. On Christmas Day of 1941, Hong Kong fell to the Japanese. Governor Mark Young had holed himself up at the Peninsula Hotel on Kowloon where the Japanese found him and sent him off to Manchuria as a prisoner.

Hong Kong was liberated in August, 1945 when the Union Jack went back above government buildings and back on other government property and all three territories of Hong Kong were once again recognized as a British Crown Colony.

Four years later, in 1949, came the fall of the Republic of China (ROC) to communism by the revolution of Mao Tse-tung. That caused hundreds of thousands of Chinese pouring into Hong Kong, escaping communist rule to live in the small British enclave. It was an influx unparalleled in its history. Hong Kong was not a 100% degree of security since Mao Tse-tung proclaimed that the two long-ago treaties of perpetuity for Great Britain were forced on China and unrecognized by the government he founded: The People's Republic of China (PRC). History was not on his side, but geography was. With the People's Liberation Army above Boundary Street of the New Territories, the leadership of the People's Republic of China could choose the time for the disregard of words and signatures. Likely times of a takeover by China were suspected including 1997 when the lease of the New Territories would end, but it was one of many suspects of the PRC's ambitions. It was just as likely as any time or that the government of the People's Republic of China might be a fallen government by then, or if it was still intact in 1997, maybe its leader of that year would be honorable and lead a democracy and that the new leader would want to keep the word and signature of the past. Most Hong Kong People tried not to have their minds dwell on Mao and life north of Boundary Street.

By 1960 the population of Hong Kong had swelled to three million, almost all refugees from China.

In 1967 came the Cultural Revolution in China with Red Guards and a militia of 300 Chinese soldiers from the People's Liberation Army (PLA) with automatic rifles crossing into Hong Kong territory. The British Government had an aircraft ready at Kai Tak Airport to take Governor David Trench and his family to safety should the PLA and Red Guards get too close to raising their flags over Hong Kong.

In 1975, with the fall of South Vietnam, some 57,000 Vietnamese refugees started pouring into Hong Kong on makeshift boats, and those whose vessels made it were accepted by Hong Kong as their destination of first refuge.

A poll of Hong Kong People in 1982 was taken with 95% of the respondents wanting the political status of Hong Kong to remain maintained by the United Kingdom.

On September the 22nd of 1982 the Prime Minister of the United Kingdom, Margaret Thatcher was in Beijing, capital of the People's Republic of China, to negotiate the future of the New Territories with Chairman Deng Xiaoping of the People's Republic of China. She felt the time was right since she could deal from a position of strength as well as a time of necessity. The strength came from her recent victory in the Falkland Islands after Argentina's invasion, and the necessity was that mortgages in the New Territories covered fifteen year spans, and fifteen years from 1982 was 1997, the year the lease of the New Territories would be ended if not renewed. No leases had been granted covering any dates beyond June 27, 1997, three days prior to handover. This travel of Prime Minister Thatcher was the first time a sitting British Prime Minister had ever been to China.

On September the 24th, two days after her arrival, Prime Minister Thatcher met with Deng Xiaoping. As expected, Prime Minister Thatcher's position was that the lease of the New Territories should be extended.

To the Prime Minister, although more than mindful that Deng had the additional seizure of Hong Kong Island and Kowloon on his mind, those two territories were not issues as Hong Kong Island and Kowloon were the property of Great Britain in perpetuity by virtue of the two treaties in which China ceded those lands.

Deng Xiaoping's position was that Hong Kong Island, the Kowloon Peninsula, and the lease of the New Territories were "unequal" (meaning a result of treaties signed under duress). Deng's Foreign Office released the statement, "Hong Kong is part of Chinese territory. The treaties concerning the Hong Kong area between the British Government and the Government of the Manchu Dynasty of China were unequal treaties that have never been accepted by the Chinese people. The consistent position of the Government of the People's Republic of China is not bound by these unequal treaties and that the whole of Hong Kong area will be recovered when conditions are ripe."

Prime Minister Thatcher responded that "If a country will not stand by one treaty, it will not stand by another," and that abrogating the perpetuity clauses of two of the three documents would be "very serious indeed."

Prime Minister Thatcher's only victory was that Deng agreed to allow Hong Kong to retain much of its own system for the next fifty years, until 2047. "One Country, Two Systems" was the way he defined Hong Kong's status as a Special Administrative Region (SAR). The error was in defining "One Country, Two Systems" as the system of communism for the mainland and the system of capitalism for Hong Kong. It was an error because the system of the mainland was dictatorship and the system of Hong Kong was liberty. On the mainland of China, most large urban areas were becoming highly capitalistic for the time of handover—but the people did not live in liberty. Although people cannot be free without capitalism, it is possible to have capitalism without freedom as has been proven by so many dictatorial governments. And that is just the way the government of the People's Republic of China wanted it to be maintained: a dictatorship that exalts one party, one government, and one race.

Prime Minister Thatcher went from Beijing to Hong Kong where most of Hong Kong's press had already received the news from Xinhua, the PRC's official news agency, that "the Chinese government's position on the recovery of the whole region of Hong Kong is unequivocal and known to all."

Prime Minister Thatcher told the Hong Kong people that Britain had "a moral responsibility" to Hong Kong and that Great Britain takes that responsibility "very, very seriously." Those words didn't help with Hong Kong people. For the first time since Hong Kong had become a British Crown Colony, the majority of Hong Kong people mistrusted Great Britain.

The degree of mistrust increased during two years of negotiations.

They went Deng's way.

Almost two years to the day since the Thatcher-Deng meeting, on September 26, 1984 the negotiated Joint Declaration between Great Britain and the People's Republic of China was released: There was not an extended 99 lease for the New Territories; and the whole of Hong Kong, meaning Hong Kong Island, Kowloon, and the New Territories would be turned over to the People's Republic of China when the lease on the New Territories would run out. The Joint Declaration called for the People's Republic of China to take over all three entities on July 1, 1997 with those three entities under "one country, two systems" with Hong Kong, Kowloon, and the New Territories able to have the status of Special Administrative Region of the People's Republic of China for fifty years more, until 2047. The designation of "A" standing for "Administrative" rather than "Autonomous" was carefully done since the word "Autonomous" was used in the 17 Point document with Tibet in 1951, and Tibet's lack of autonomy was, by this time, world-known.

The Joint Declaration of 1984 between Great Britain and the People's Republic of China was filled with guaranteeing language including that Hong Kong People would retain for 50 years what they have and that the "rights and freedoms, including those of the person, of speech, of the press, of assembly, of association, of travel, of movement, of correspondence, of strike, of choice of occupation, of academic research and of religious belief, will be ensured by law..." (But the Constitution of the People's Republic of China, itself, gave nearly all the same guarantees to its own people and those guarantees were not observed.)

Prior to the realization that Great Britain would be leaving Hong Kong, demonstrations were virtually unknown in Hong Kong but just before Christmas of 1988 there was a demonstration close by the Star Ferry Pier across from Kowloon on the harbor's Hong Kong Island's side. All the posters and placards that the demonstrators carried were hand-made:

"Sir David Ford, the dear Chief Secretary—While you and your British buddies can wave 'bye-bye' to Hong Kong in 1997 or earlier, returning to your London homes to enjoy more 'fish and chips and tea' we, and our sons and daughters, and theirs, are going to remain in our Hong Kong homes. Therefore if you cannot support us nor are concerned about Hong Kong people's struggle for democracy and freedom after 1997, would you please stop making stupid statements and shut up when you have nothing to say? We, the great Hong Kong people will be accountable and responsible to the history of Hong Kong, our home!"

"The future of five and one half million Hong Kong people is not in the USA, Canada, Australia, New Zealand and other immigration havens, but right where we are."

"You're going to go home in 1997 and have tea and crumpets, and we're going to be here and we want our freedom."

"The two hottest collector's items in Hong Kong after 1997 are democracy and freedom. Have you saved some for your children yet? If you don't support democracy and freedom now, can you look your children and your grandchildren in their faces later, knowing you could have done something now however small?"

"Tea and Sympathy? Have tea, Sir David, but where's your sympathy for Hong Kong people?"

Then came June 4, 1989 and the massacre of Tiananmen Square in Beijing. Any optimism at all—and there wasn't much—was smothered. No event had ever shaken the people of Hong Kong as that one did. Massive demonstrations with somewhere between 500,000 and one million Hong Kong people protested the massacre. This was out of a population of about 5.7 million at the time. A huge replica of the Goddess of Democracy was erected in Victoria Park, shortly after the one built by the students in Beijing was destroyed. The Hong Kong demonstrations against the People's Republic of China went on and on and on through sunsets and sunrises. (That anniversary has been observed in Hong Kong every year since 1989, most organized by Hong Kong Legislative Council Member Szeto Wah during the rest of his lifetime.)

Four months after the Tiananmen Square Massacre, with protests against the People's Republic of China still on high, Governor David Wilson advised Hong Kong people to use their rights and freedoms "with self-restraint."

On April 4, 1990, The Basic Law (a Constitution for Hong Kong) was established by the People's Republic of China for the years 1997-2047. It is a document of 160 Articles which is a more detailed and somewhat changed itemized guarantee of the freedoms and autonomy promised Hong Kong in the Joint Declaration written by Great Britain and the PRC. It has been referred to by democracy advocates not as "The Basic Law" but as "The Basic Flaw."

On July 9, 1992 a new Governor came to Hong Kong. He was the 28th sent by the Crown: The Right Honourable Christopher Francis Patten. He started a surprising and unparalleled administration as the most outspoken of any Governor of Hong Kong for democracy while walking a tight-rope stretched between the people of Hong Kong and his home government in London, and the People's Republic of China.

The Government of the People's Republic of China was outraged at his "outlandish, audacious and criminal behavior," and much of the business community of Hong Kong placed itself on the PRC's side, scared to death of the displeasure of that oncoming government.

Governor Patten hit back at the business community; "This is one of the most sophisticated economic communities in the world, well-traveled, well educated, hugely successful economically. There are some people who think it's outlandish that they want to decide how their kids should be educated, who should collect the dustbins, how much of their taxes should go on housing rather than health service. I mean it's crazy. What we have to do now is to try and convince the business community that accountable government and the beginnings of democratization aren't a threat to five and one half percent growth, low taxes, big surpluses, and a pro-business ethic in government. I, too, hope we will be able to make at least some progress in convincing Chinese leaders that this hugely precious community, representing as it does twenty-three percent of Chinese GNP, succeeds not just because of some capitalist equation but because its way of life helps to sustain its prosperity as well as its prosperity helping to sustain its way of life."

The Government of the People's Republic of China's voice was loud and clear. It announced that come July 1, 1997, the first day of handover, they may well not honor contracts made with Hong Kong prior to the takeover, and they would abolish all three tiers of Hong Kong Government established before July 1, 1997.

Beijing, never subtle with language, continually called Governor Patten "a criminal" and decided not to deal with him but rather to deal with his second in command, Hong Kong's Chief Secretary Anson Chan. She was much more palatable to Beijing. In time, representatives from the People's Republic of China would not even shake hands with the Governor, and any invitation to Beijing was addressed not to the Governor but to Anson Chan. By such treatment they were attempting to send a message to the people of Hong Kong that the Governor had no authority with the Beijing Government. Many Hong Kong people had felt betrayed by Great Britain and were especially resentful that Hong Kong people were given no voice in the negotiations. But they knew, and some admitted, that the People's Republic of China held all the cards, geographically as well as militarily, and in terms of the water and food supplied to Hong Kong by China, Prime Minister Thatcher had few credible threats over the People's Republic of China. Other than democracy activists of Hong Kong led by Legislators Martin

Lee Chu-ming and Szeto Wah, many public Hong Kong leaders felt there were no roads open to fight and win against the will of the People's Republic of China.

One of the most unexpected events in the Pre-1997 chronology occurred in October, 1995 with the statement of Governor Christopher Patten calling on his nation, Great Britain, to give the right of abode to all the 3.3 million Hong Kong residents who qualify for passports. Home Secretary Michael Howard quickly said it would not be done. Unsurprisingly, Governor Patten's advocacy received the praise of many Hong Kong people. There was no praise from most of the business community who gave the Governor their disapproval of such a suggestion, and there were new epithets given him from the People's Republic of China who, even more markedly, turned their back on him with the claim that he is "irrelevant." The PRC announced that during the transition period "the last colonial governor cannot represent Britain."

Governor Patten said, "After this is over" on July the First of 1997, "I'm certain I'm going to have earned some time with a good book under a tree."

No one fought him on that one.

And so it happened, and the phrase "One Country, Two Systems" was inaugurated in Hong Kong on the midnight that separated June the 30th from July the First of 1997.

Hong Kong was to exist as an SAR: a Special Administrative Region of the People's Republic of China for 50 years, permitting within that period of July the First of 1997 through July the First of 2047, more liberties than anywhere else under the government of the PRC. The obvious unanswered question (and even most unasked) is, “What happens on July the First of 2047?”

There might well be a strong answer—not a good one but a strong one—and it has to do with Taiwan:

From its takeover of China forward, the People’s Republic of China has had a public obsession in governing Taiwan’s territory. There was little doubt that the PRC’s plan was to encourage Taiwan that a SAR status works for the people of Hong Kong with the SAR status having many of its own laws rather than all those laws that apply to the rest of China. In short, the message was that the SAR is for Hong Kong People and for the international community of business and tourists to see that (on the surface, at least,) Hong Kong appears to be very much as it was under the British.

It could then be that the PRC’s fixation of some plan to rule Taiwan could be realized before 2047 through negotiations to make it a Special Administrative Region. Going further, with the dawn of July the First of 2047 both Hong Kong and Taiwan could then be under the total jurisdiction of the PRC and the PRC could decree that all provinces and territories under the PRC’s domain must live under the laws and rules of all other provinces and cities of the People’s Republic of China.

By the PRC’s definition that would be known as Deng Xiaoping’s 2047.

CHAPTER SEVEN

MOST OFTEN REPORTED AND TAUGHT: (DECEMBER 15, 1978 FORWARD) "U.S. POLICY IS CORRECT IN REGARDING TAIWAN AS A PROVINCE OF THE PEOPLE'S REPUBLIC OF CHINA"

THE TRUTH:

ONLY IF THE HISTORIES OF THE PEOPLE'S REPUBLIC OF CHINA AND TAIWAN ARE TOTALLY DISREGARDED

Since Revolution Day of October the First of 1949 every consecutive leader of the People's Republic of China (PRC) from Chairman Mao Tse-tung [Mao Zedong] all the way to 2012's General Secretary Xi Jinping has proclaimed that Taiwan is a renegade province of the People's Republic of China. For sure, at different historical times, Taiwan came under the jurisdiction of Emperors of China, then, briefly, the Republic (not the People's Republic) of China (ROC), and under the jurisdiction of Portugal, the jurisdiction of Spain, the jurisdiction of the Netherlands, the jurisdiction of Japan, and now Taiwan is under the jurisdiction of its own people—but in that long history the flag of the People's Republic of China has not flown for one minute over Taiwan, and the Taiwanese have not for one minute sung the National Anthem of the People's Republic of China or for one minute adopted the government of the People's Republic of China or for one minute accepted the system of the People's Republic of China.

It would make as much sense for Prime Minister David Cameron to call the United States of America a renegade province of the United Kingdom. More logically, Prime Minister Shinzo Abe of Japan could say Taiwan is a renegade province of Japan since a treaty was signed by Li Hung-chang for the Emperor of China in the Treaty of Shimonoseki in 1895 giving Taiwan to Japan in perpetuity—forever—and Japan kept it for fifty years until the end of World War II. But neither of those two fates will happen because Great Britain and Japan are democracies—and democracies care more about the will of the people rather than expansion of their territory. In a more current example, in 2014 Great Britain encouraged a vote of the people of Scotland to determine to either stay in the United Kingdom or for Scotland to become an independent nation. [Scotland voted to stay with the United Kingdom.] Scotland has a population of only five million, not 23 million as does Taiwan. The People's Republic of China opposes having a free vote of the Taiwanese to make such a decision—and the government of the United States of America also opposes such a vote by the people of Taiwan.

Taiwan is a free society; whose democracy of 23 million people compose more people than three-quarters of the individual countries in the United Nations Organization—from which it was ejected. In Taiwan's case a democracy does not only mean free, fair, and frequent elections but all the foundations of democracy: a separate executive branch, legislative branch, judicial branch; freedom of the press, speech, religion, assembly. Everything.

The People's Republic of China has none of them. But not only that. The PRC has given nuclear technology and missile technology to both Iran and North Korea. The PRC has 157 nuclear warheads and it is manufacturing 120 new Intercontinental Ballistic Missiles, half of them for ocean-going warfare. Why? Who threatens an attack on that nation? In 2015 the PRC increased its military budget 17.8% while the PRC has continued to embrace governments hostile to the United States not only including Iran and North Korea, but also Venezuela and Sudan. In 2015 a fleet of PRC warships docked in Iran for Joint Naval Exercises including a crew of 650 and a guided missile destroyer. These exercises were broadcast by the PRC as "establishing peace, stability, tranquility, and multilateral mutual cooperation." No surprise. The PRC was the only national supporter of Pol Pot's Khmer Rouge genocide of Cambodia.

And, significantly, the PRC killed American troops in Korea and Vietnam. Yet the U.S. Government caters to the People's Republic of China while shunning, criticizing, and isolating the democracy of Taiwan, treating it as a pariah.

An example: On April the 20th, 2006 President Hu Jintao of the People's Republic of China was greeted on the South Lawn of the White House by President Bush (43) with both Presidents giving speeches, the playing of the PRC's national anthem, and President Hu given a twenty-one-gun salute. The following month, President Chen of Taiwan was traveling to Central America and requested a refueling and rest stop in either New York or San Francisco. Neither stop was permitted by the U.S. State Department, rejecting any transit point within the conterminous area of the United States. He was, instead, offered a refueling stop in either Alaska or Hawaii, as long as his presence was kept only at the airport with no overnight stay. President Chen rejected the rather humiliating offer. Later President Chen made another trip to Central America and this time, thankfully, President Bush intervened with the State Department and President Chen's plane was allowed to have refueling stops in California. However, he could not venture further than the airports. The policy stays intact that the President of Taiwan and/or Taiwanese officials cannot visit with our President or other officials of our government, nor can Taiwan's President have more than refueling stops in the United States with overnight stops at the airport if requested and granted.

With apologies for its length, the following is a chronological history of the People's Republic of China that is vital to know in any discussion regarding Taiwan. It isn't ancient history. It was October the 1st of 1949 when the communist revolution of Mao Tse-tung succeeded in taking over China from the government of the Republic of China (ROC). That was when the name was changed to the People's Republic of China rather than the Republic of China; the system was changed to communism; the flag was changed; the anthem was changed; the government was changed; everything was changed. And the vanquished government led by Chiang Kai-Scheck fled to Taiwan, 95 miles across the Taiwan Strait, with over one million of his followers.

Mao Tse-tung said that the People's Republic of China represents the legal government of China including Taiwan—and the PRC will take Taiwan. At the same time Chiang Kai-Shek of the Republic of China said that the Republic of China represents the legal government of China and the ROC is going to take back the mainland. Since both of them couldn't represent China, the United States adopted a One-China Policy recognizing the non-communist government of the Republic of China, not the People's Republic of China. After all, Chiang Kai-shek's government of the Republic was an ally in World War II that had just concluded four years earlier and it was one of the five founders of the United Nations.

Taiwan was not a democracy back then but few countries were democracies back then. Only around 24 democracies existed in the entire world. Chiang Kai-shek was a dictator not representing the majority of Taiwanese but the alternative was the dictatorship of Mao Tse-tung whose communism represented few if any in Taiwan.

With all that as background, the U.S chose to retain diplomatic relations with the Republic of China on Taiwan, not the People's Republic of China. And so did most of the free-world nations.

And the U.S. held to that policy of recognition of Taiwan through the administrations of Truman, Eisenhower, Kennedy, Johnson, Nixon, and Ford. When President Nixon had travelled to China in 1972, he visited with Chairman Mao Tse-tung and Premier Chou En-lai and was told the People's Republic of China wanted diplomatic relations with the United States under three conditions. The demand of the PRC was for the United States to break relations with the government on Taiwan, get all the U.S. troops out of Taiwan, and abrogate—break the 1954 created Mutual Defense Treaty between the U.S. and Taiwan. President Nixon instantly, within a second, said, "No."

In 1975 the PRC gave the same offer to President Ford with the same three conditions. He said "no."

Then came President Carter. When he was given the same three conditions he said, "yes."

On December the 15th of 1978 President Carter addressed the nation surprisingly to announce the United States of America was switching diplomatic relations from the non-communist government of Taiwan to the communist government of the People's Republic of China. Without publically itemizing the three conditions he accepted, he had, indeed, accepted them. If to no one else, it was obvious to those who were aware of the three conditions.

Former President Nixon was privately furious. He believed that a former president should never publicly criticize a sitting president—and, therefore, he didn't. He believed that if he had anything to say to a sitting president, a former president should give that criticism privately—and he did: On December the 20th, five days after President Carter's speech, Former President of the United States Nixon sent a long letter to President Carter, respectful, but he left no question as to where he stood. Near the end of the letter he wrote, "I have not written it for the record and I do not intend to make it public."

The December the 15th date of 1978 as the date of President Carter's speech is important since he chose to give the speech ten days before Christmas while the Congress was on Christmas vacation. Many members of that Congress from both major political parties were privately and publically angry, and when they returned to D.C. they wrote and passed the Taiwan Relations Act of 1979 calling for U.S. military supplies if Taiwan were to need them. Senator Goldwater brought President Carter's abrogation of our treaty with Taiwan through the courts all the way to the Supreme Court but the Supreme Court refused to hear it, as usual not wanting to get into a dispute between the other two branches of government. In addition, this was an international matter falling under the umbrella of the President's foreign policy.

Advance the calendar to a very important date: May the First of 1991. By this time Chiang Kai-Schek of Taiwan had died, his son, Chiang Ching-kuo had became President and had died and Vice President Lee Teng-hui was now President. On that first day of 1991's May, President Lee said that "Taiwan is not the legal government of China. We do not claim China. We are Taiwan, period." He not only advocated but brought about a full absolute, multi-party democracy. He was from the old one-party system—the Kuomintang Party—but in time he and the Kuomintang disowned each other. After all, he brought about the abolition of the one-party system that had kept his party in office so long. Democracy, of course, is always the enemy of a one-party system.

Now advance the calendar:

President Chen of the Democratic Progressive Party had been the president since 2000, and in his second term he wanted a vote of the people to choose whether or not they wanted to change the name of the country from the Republic of China—to Taiwan. It was justifiably thought by many that the United States would be for it since the U.S. claimed a "One China Policy" and since 1991 Taiwan had made no claims on China. But the U.S. was against such a free vote, and our State Department warned President Chen that he should not have such a referendum. Moreover, the United States Government opposed and continues to oppose many democratic processes for Taiwan since democratic processes would change the Status Quo.

Taiwan, with or without permission of the U.S. or the PRC took the word "China" out from a number of some state enterprises such as the Post office and the Petroleum Company; but the U.S. State Department was even opposed to those changes. The State Department wanted to leave the word "China" in, as its use enhanced the U.S. policy that Taiwan is a renegade province of China.

Talwan's President Chen wanted to hold a plebiscite to see if the people of Taiwan wanted to change the Constitution from one that was written by a dictatorship years back into one proclaiming democracy. As expected, the U.S. State Department said not to do that. However, with good reason the United States praised Iraqis for going to the polls to change their constitution from one that was written under a dictatorship to a democracy. Beyond moral consistency, the State Department warned Taiwan—"don't do it." The Status Quo applied only to Taiwan.

When incidents changed with severe actions taken by the PRC against Taiwan, the State Department didn't warn that the Status-Quo was being changed by the PRC: On March 14 of 2005, a law of China was passed stating that if Taiwan should make steps toward formal independence, non-peaceful means would be used against Taiwan. In recent years China has had 11 amphibious rehearsals of an invasion of Taiwan, one of the most recent with the collaboration of Russian troops and over 30 land War Games in 2005 opposite the Taiwan Strait.

In China, just across that 95 mile Strait of water from Taiwan, there were or are 375,000 Chinese troops stationed as well as 700 combat aircraft. Most ominously, China has been increasing its deployment of missiles targeted on Taiwan from just across the Strait at a rate of about two new missiles a week. By 2015 the estimated number reached 1700 while the U.S. Government did not and does not accuse China of breaking the Status-Quo for any of that.

Other nations see all this and they correctly assume there is a giant exception to our pursuit of liberty. After all, a dictatorship and one of the worst human rights violators in the world is given the handshake of the United States while Taiwan's democratic procedures are condemned.

They also see that Kosovo has a population of only some two million people, yet and justifiably—the U.S. Government has endorsed Kosovo's independence from Serbia. Those opposed to its independence were Serbia, Russia, Cypress, the United Nations, and the People's Republic of China.

They also see that Saddam Hussein claimed Kuwait was the

19th province of Iraq and Saddam Hussein invaded and took Kuwait—by force and held it until the U.S. and its coalition of allies liberated Kuwait's independence—but the U.S. opposes independence for Taiwan.

They also see that in 2014 Vladimir Putin of Russia took Crimea by force from Ukraine and in 2015 he has been targeting Eastern Ukraine as a part of Russia.

They also know that President Nixon's 1972 trip to China was intended to create "triangulation" between the United States and the Soviet Union and China so that never again would the USSR and the PRC become allied together against the United States and its interests. And now in 2015 Russia and the PRC have increased their alliance toward a pre-1972 level.

They also see that the PRC is reclaiming land from the South China Sea to build military bases on the Spratly Islands claimed by five other nations; Brunei, Malaysia, the Philippines, Taiwan, and Vietnam. The PRC is making further claims on the Paracel Islands from Taiwan and Vietnam, and the Senkaku Islands in the East China Sea from Japan and Taiwan.

Their take-overs, including their ultimate objective of taking Taiwan, is not a lust for a bigger population. They have gone through such primitive means to limit their biggest-in-the-world population so the PRC certainly has no need for 23,000,000 more people. Their lust is for more territory, much of it for military advances.

Abdicating such territory to the PRC by world powers, including by the United States, is nothing less than waving a white flag.

It should be remembered that far from China, on December the 17th of 2010 in Tunisia, a young man chose self-immolation because police took away his vegetable cart while he was selling his vegetables from the cart without a license to use it. It was the tragic incident that started the ill-conceived Arab Spring. This was highlighted by President Obama saying that because of that self-immolation, it was time for the President of Tunisia, Ben-Ali to leave office—and he did leave office. What President Obama didn't say, nor did he ever complain that the PRC under the then-current Administration of Hu Jintao, witnessed over 200 Tibetans who committed self-immolation because of wanting freedom of religion; Tibetan Buddhism. Why did President Obama blame Ben-Ali of Tunisia and not Hu Jintao of the PRC? Likely it was no fear of Ben-Ali but fear of making such comment against Hu Jintao.

The official United States policy toward Taiwan is best known through State Department communications from January the First of 1979. The following was given by telephone and some paraphrasing may have taken place from fast writing, but the substance was as written here: Meetings with officials from Taiwan cannot take place in State Department buildings nor the White House Complex including the Executive Office Building. Meetings are not permitted to attend functions held at the Washington residence of Taiwan's representative to the U.S. or U.S. Embassies. It is not permitted to refer to Taiwan's authorities as a "government" but as "Taiwan authorities." It is not permitted to refer by the term "Taiwanese" but requires instead to say "people on Taiwan." It is not permitted to go to National Day celebrations of Taiwan. The U.S. does not recognize Taiwan as a "sovereign independent country" and "the U.S. does not allow the flag of Taiwan to fly on U.S. Government premises." The U.S. does not support Taiwan's "membership in international organizations that require statehood." We have a "One China policy."

It is most likely that such a U.S. policy is or will be a danger to world-wide democracy and to the United States itself.

CHAPTER EIGHT

MOST OFTEN REPORTED AND TAUGHT: (1967 Forward) "A TWO-STATE SOLUTION; ISRAEL AND AN ARAB PALESTINIAN STATE IS THE BEST FUTURE OF THE LAND NOW CALLED ISRAEL"

THE TRUTH:

THAT IS NOT BASED ON HISTORY NOR IS IT BASED ON LOGIC. IT IS PRIMARILY BASED ON THE UNAWARE AND BY THOSE WHO WOULD LIKE TO SEE THE END OF ISRAEL

On May the 19th of 2011 in a major address to the people of the world, President of the United States Barack Obama stated, "We believe the borders of Israel and Palestine should be based on the 1967 lines with mutually agreed swaps, so that secure and recognized borders are established for both States."

Unprecedented.

That statement regarding the 1967 lines is one of the worst, if not the very worst statement made by any U.S. President regarding a friendly nation that won a war.

Not even North Vietnam, a foe of the United States, has ever been told by a U.S. President to go back to the 1975 lines (in its case). Never. In 1975 North Vietnam won the territory of South Vietnam after over 58,000 Americans lost their lives to help the South Vietnamese retain their nation. In the years since the defeat, neither the United States nor any other nation has told North Vietnam to "give up that territory." There has been not one resolution to that effect offered in the United Nations. Instead, most countries of the world, including the United States, gave diplomatic relations and trade agreements with the Socialist Republic of Vietnam which is what had been known as North and South Vietnam.

In keeping with President Obama's Middle East policy, should the United States base its borders on the 1846 lines with Mexico? Or, for that matter base its lines of territory on the 1775 lines with Great Britain? How about with mutually agreed swaps?

What makes that line of his speech even more absurd is that a Palestinian State did not exist in 1967—or any year—but certainly what he conveyed was that there was such a State in 1967.

Since, at the time of the President's speech, some 44 years had passed since the war, many people either forgot or never knew what happened back in 1967; some hadn't been born then or were too young to remember while some never learned the facts or simply forgot the facts in all the time that had passed.

Instead of what the President said, the war had nothing to do with the borders of the State of Israel and an Arab State called Palestine. It had, instead, everything to do with the imminent invasion from Arab States for the purpose of exterminating Israel:

On May the 18th of 1967, the Voice of the Arabs Radio broadcast that President Gamal Abdul Nasser of Egypt announced: "The sole method we shall apply against Israel is a total war which will result in the extermination of Zionist existence."

On May the 20th President Nasser instituted a blockade of the Gulf of Eilat so that no shipping could move in or out of Israel through the Red Sea.

On the same date President Nasser's tanks started going eastward through the Sinai Desert toward Israel. Standing in the way of the tanks within the Sinai were the U.N. Emergency Force Peacekeepers. President Nasser asked Secretary General of the United Nations U Thant to remove the peacekeeping force as Nasser's tanks were about to invade Israel. In a move that defeated the purpose and even defeated the definition of a peacekeeping effort, Secretary General U Thant accommodated President Nasser and removed the U.N. Emergency Force Peacekeepers so President Nasser would be undeterred in launching his invasion.

On May the 27th Nasser said, "Our basic objective will be the destruction of Israel. The Arab people want to fight."

On May the 29th Nasser said, "We have reached the stage of serious action and not declarations."

On May the 30th Nasser said, "The armies of Egypt, Jordan, Syria and Lebanon are poised on the borders of Israel." Additionally, President Nasser stated publically that he had "received the commitment of Iraq's President Aref who announced, 'Our goal is clear—to wipe Israel off the map.'"

As May ended and June began, Nasser rejected a plea from the United States and European nations to "allow freedom of shipping in the Gulf of Aqaba" so war could be prevented. [The name, the Gulf of Aqaba is used in Arab nations while the name, the Gulf of Eilat is used in Israel. It's the same place.]

It is important to remember that the planned attack was not for the Sinai, not for the Gaza Strip, not for the Golan Heights, not for East Jerusalem, and not for Judea and Samaria. Since 1948 Egypt already had Sinai and the Gaza Strip, Syria already had the Golan Heights, Jordan already had East Jerusalem and had Judea and Samaria, having renamed those territories as their West Bank. All of this held as theirs in the preceding 19 years since 1948.

Israel was confident that at a minimum, Egypt's President Nasser and Syria's President Nureddin al-Atassi would order the invasion by their armed forces in a two-front war against Israel; Egypt from the south-west and Syria from the north. Israel's greatest concern was that Jordan would join them from the east in an attack for a three-front war.

Prime Minister Levi Eshkol of Israel wanted to guarantee to King Hussein of Jordan that if the King would just "sit on his hands and do nothing" when Egypt and Syria go to war against Israel, rather than join those two countries, "Israel will not attack or take one inch of any territory Jordan considers to be a part of its nation, including what Jordan calls its West Bank." But direct dialogue between Israel and Jordan was out of the question since diplomatic relations did not exist between them. Since Prime Minister Eshkol could not directly deliver the message to King Hussein, he communicated with the U.S. Ambassador to Israel, Ambassador Walworth Barbour, to see if he or Ambassador Findley Burns, Jr. the U.S. Ambassador to the Hashemite Kingdom of Jordan, would deliver Israel's message to King Hussein. [The United States had diplomatic relations with both Israel and Jordan.]

Ambassador Barbour did what all good U.S. Ambassadors do: he cabled the U.S. Secretary of State. The U.S. Secretary of State Dean Rusk brought the message to President Johnson.

President Johnson did one better than delegating Ambassador Barbour or Ambassador Burns to see King Hussein. He sent Under

Secretary of State for Political Affairs Eugene Rostow from Washington, D.C. to be the President's personal envoy to visit with the King of Jordan and deliver a personal message from the President.

Secretary Rostow told King Hussein of Israel's guarantee if the King would just "sit on his hands" rather than add a third front to the war against Israel. Secretary Rostow then added something more: not only did Israel make that guarantee if Jordan would not enter the war against Israel but President Johnson wanted King Hussein to know that the United States would also guarantee that Israel would not take one inch of what Jordan considered to be its territory. "There is a promise of absolute immunity," Secretary Rostow told the King.

King Hussein gave no answer. At that time of his 31st year of life, the King wanted consent for such a decision, in this case permission from other Arab leaders including from Egypt's President Nasser.

He didn't get it.

On Sunday, June the 4th, Egypt's Intelligence Agency informed Nasser of its analysis that Israel was getting ready to launch an attack on Egypt to preempt Egypt's planned invasion. In detail, Nasser was told that Israel was moving assault units and equipment to Eilat on the Gulf of Aqaba to stage that attack and they had observed that almost half of Israel's landing craft were being sent there.

Egypt's Intelligence Agency was correct in its assessment that the Israeli military was preparing Eilat. It was a logical site since Eilat was at the southern tip of the triangle of Israel between both Egypt and Jordan. On that southern tip of Israel, about four miles to Eilat's west was Taba in the Sinai of Egypt, and three miles to Eilat's east was Aqaba in Jordan. From Eilat, Israel could attack in either or both directions.

In response to the Egyptian intelligence report, Nasser ordered his combatants from the Mediterranean to come down to reinforce Arab naval strength in the Straits of Tiran off the coast of Eilat. But although the Israeli military was preparing Eilat, it was not being prepared as a launching site for attack. The buildup in Eilat was being prepared as a decoy.

With an invasion of Israel having been announced by Egypt and by Syria and other Arab nations, and with Egyptian tanks coming across the Sinai toward Israel and with the Gulf of Eilat having been blockaded, Egypt was setting the time and place for the war. That was something Israel knew that, if allowed, Israel would likely not win. Victory could more likely be achieved if Israel could set the time and place. And so it did.

On June the 5th Israel launched a preemptive strike, not from Eilat on Taba or Aqaba but from other sites in Israel targeting all of Egypt's airfields simultaneously, destroying almost the entire Air Force of Egypt, and striking Syrian and Iraqi military airfields while Israeli ground units began moving into the Gaza Strip and into the Sinai.

Israel was leaving Jordan alone, including leaving the West Bank untouched and immune in the hope Jordan would "sit on its hands" as Secretary Rostow had offered King Hussein.

At the end of that first day of war King Hussein did not sit on his hands. Instead, the King's troops attacked Israel from the West Bank and East Jerusalem. Israel responded in moments by moving troops into Jordanian-held West Bank cities of Janin, Nablus, and the Jordanian-held sector of Jerusalem.

Six days after the war began, the war was over. All parties in the Mideast agreed to a U.N. cease-fire. It was apparent that Israel could have gone on to Cairo in Egypt, Damascus in Syria, and Amman in Jordan, but Israel accommodated the call for a cease-fire of the U.N. and, particularly, the encouragement of the United States to accept it since Israel had attained what they believed were now secure borders.

In those six days of war Israel had taken both the Gaza Strip and the entire Sinai Desert up to the Suez Canal from Egypt, and had taken the Golan Heights from Syria, and had taken all of Judea and Samaria (the West Bank) from Jordan including the Jordanian-held sector of Jerusalem.

Some two decades later, during the Reagan Administration, Eugene Rostow said that "the West Bank would still be held by Jordan today if King Hussein had accepted the offer from the U.S. and Israel."

But war's casualties were high, going into the tens of thousands including 34 Americans who were not killed by Egyptians or Syrians or Jordanians, but by Israelis who mistook the U.S. ship which was off the coast of Sinai over 100 miles from the other ships of the U.S. Sixth Fleet, for a Soviet vessel aiding Egypt.

Because those Arab governments lost the war, they were too devastated and humiliated to claim their loss was due to Israel's armed forces. They chose to blame the more powerful United States for the defeat of the Arab governments. In making that claim, even Arab nations that were not militarily involved in the war severed diplomatic relations with the United States.

On June the 19th of 1967 President Johnson stated that going back to the pre-war borders as some Arab States were demanding, was "not a prescription for peace, but for renewed hostilities." But assume that what President Johnson said should be disregarded and, instead, borders should be based on the 1967 lines as President Obama has given as U.S. policy in 2011: Whether President Obama knew it or not, and maybe he didn't know it, that would not mean giving the territories to an Arab Palestinian State as President Obama suggested, but it would mean giving back the West Bank to the Hashemite Kingdom of Jordan that had invaded and seized it back in 1948 and it would mean giving the Gaza Strip back to Egypt who had invaded and took jurisdiction over it also back in 1948, neither nation even wanting those territories in years following the 1967 War for the following reasons:

Three years after the 1967 war, Jordan's King Hussein fought a war not from a threat from Israel but from a war against the Palestine Liberation Organization (PLO) of Yasser Arafat who wanted to take over Jordan.

[The PLO wanted to take over all of Jordan as well as what Jordan had called the West Bank but had once again been named Judea and Samaria since it was back in Israel's hands since winning the 1967 war.] The PLO was aided by Syria and Iraq; a war in which King Hussein's Jordanian troops killed an estimated 10,000 members and supporters of the PLO and drove Yasser Arafat to Lebanon where he started "a State within a State."

During that war King Hussein requested aid from the United States, Great Britain, and from Israel, with all three nations accommodating King Hussein. During his lifetime, King Hussein survived 12 assassination attempts by what were becoming referred to as Arab Palestinians.

Egypt was also disillusioned with Arab Palestinians, and in 1978 President Anwar Sadat at Camp David talks with U.S. President Carter and Israel's Prime Minister Begin, Sadat made no demand to have the Gaza Strip once again under Egypt's jurisdiction.

Instead, he agreed to an ambiguous future autonomy. There was never any secret that due to so many of Gaza's radical inhabitants and its leadership, President Sadat considered the Gaza Strip a territorial burden rather than a prized Egyptian jurisdiction. [It was three rulers earlier when Egyptian King Farouk had seized control of the Gaza Strip in the 1948 War.] Sadat had been stuck with it.

Throughout the Obama Administration, the U.S. Government called the West Bank and the Gaza Strip as land "occupied by Israel." In his major speech on the Middle East given on May the 19th of 2011 President Obama once more spoke of Israel as an occupier. He said, "The dream of a Jewish and democratic State cannot be fulfilled with permanent occupation."

The obvious question was how the Arab Palestinians in the West Bank and the Gaza Strip could claim their land was occupied when they never had that land? It was a question never referred to by President Obama as he persisted in calling it an Israeli occupation. Before the June War of 1967 when Egypt had jurisdiction over the Gaza Strip and Jordan had taken the West Bank, neither Egypt nor Jordan were called "occupiers." During their nineteen years of jurisdiction neither Egypt nor Jordan would allow its citizens to even mention the words, "Independent Palestinian State."

Before Jordan and Egypt, Great Britain had jurisdiction over that land. And before that it was under the jurisdiction of the Ottoman Empire of Turkey. And before that was the time of the Crusades and before that Rome ruled it. And that takes the calendar back to Biblical times prior to the time there was an Islam. [Mohammad ibn Abd Allah was born in or close to A.D. 570.]

The only period that could even be perceived as an interruption of jurisdictions was the U.N.'s designation of an Independent Arab State for portions of Judea and Samaria and Gaza, but it never came to fruition because of the instant invasion, seizure, and jurisdiction by Jordan over Judea and Samaria and by Egypt over Gaza during the quests of Jordan and Egypt to seize those territories enroute to a planned but unfulfilled seizure of all Israel.

[Palestine was never a nation but a region much as Scandinavia is not a nation but is a region containing the nations of Denmark, Norway, and Sweden. Through the years the definition of Palestine's territory went through a myriad of boundaries, partitions, and changes of borders. The original Mandate for Palestine (April 24, 1920) included what today is called Jordan, Israel, the West Bank, and Gaza. If divided into percentages the Mandate would have been 78% to Jordan, and all the rest would have been 22%. Taking away what today is called the West Bank and Gaza from Israel would then give Israel 17½%. By the time of U.N. Resolution 181 of November 29, 1947, borders had been changed to make Jordan a separate State not included in Palestine. During all this time Jordan was called Transjordan. Its name was changed in 1949 to the Hashemite Kingdom of Jordan.] Jerusalem was designated to be an international zone which Jordan did not permit.

On May 14, 1948, Israel declared its independence in compliance with the borders prescribed in U.N. Resolution 181. When Egypt and Jordan immediately took the land granted to an Independent State by the United Nations, Jordan got as far as seizing East Jerusalem and taking over Judea and Samaria. All Jews who survived the Jordanian invasion were either killed or expelled. Their graveyards were all that were left of them and so they were destroyed, with the gravestones used as latrines. Christians who remained were mandated to send their children to schools to learn the Islamic religion. Even with the failure of seizing Israel, there was triumph in Jordan's success in taking Judea, Samaria, and East Jerusalem in the 1948 War and in Egypt's jurisdiction over the Gaza

Strip, and both Jordan and Egypt retained the belief that a forthcoming war would give those Arab Nations possession of Israel-proper.

President Obama has publically opposed Israel building settlements on the West Bank. But Israel won the war. Do we insist that North Vietnam should not allow settlements of North Vietnamese in what was Saigon? Of course not. The North Vietnamese won the war. They now administer and call that city Ho Chi Minh City.

It is apparent that the term "occupation" has recently been used to describe what friends of the United States are said to do when they win wars, but not enemies of the United States are said to do when they win wars. Not just Vietnam: the State Department would later try to bring about a partition of Bosnia that had been captured in horrible acts of aggression by Slobodan Milosevic's Serbia. The U.S. did not refer to Milosevic's capture as occupied territory, but as "facing the fact that it won those territories in war."

In President Obama's May the 19th 2011 speech, he said, "The United States believes that negotiations should result in two States, with permanent Palestinian borders with Israel, Jordan, and Egypt, and permanent Israeli borders with Palestine." Assuming that Palestine is to be a State, why didn't he also say permanent Israeli borders with Jordan, Egypt, Lebanon and Syria? That does not mean he intended to leave out those borders but he was even leaving out territory on pre-war maps of 1967.

The phrase, "a two State solution with two States living side by side in peace and security" has been used in one way or another countless times by the President and spokespeople of the State Department, becoming the memorized statement to answer almost any question regarding U.S. policy toward Israel. In the General Assembly of the United Nations on September the 23rd of 2009,

President Obama said, "The goal is clear: two States living side by side in peace and security." On August the 20th of 2010 Secretary of State Hillary Clinton in a State Department Press Briefing put it this way: "The goal of two States—Israel and Palestine, living side by side in peace and security." On May the 17th of 2011 in a meeting with King Abdullah II of Jordan in the Oval Office, President Obama said, "two States that are living side by side in peace and security." But a clear indication that such a plan would not bring about peace and security is that thousands of missiles had already been launched from the Gaza Strip against Israel ever since the Gaza Strip had been completely withdrawn by Israel when Israel's Prime Minister Ariel Sharon forced out the over 9,000 Israelis who lived there in 2005 and gave the entire Gaza Strip to the Palestinian Authority in the hope it would attain that peace and security. It attained neither. During the next six years 18,000 missiles were launched from the Gaza Strip into Israel. Those missiles were sent from Iran and Syria to their surrogates of Hamas in Gaza and also to Hezbollah in Lebanon, being used as storage depots for later use against Israel.

There is a tremendous global inconsistency in U.S. foreign policy that should be apparent as the United States advocates a Two State Solution for Israel and the Palestinian Authority while in another international controversy, the U.S. advocates a One State Solution for Taiwan and the People's Republic of China. In the Middle East the State of Israel is a long-time friend of the United States and a democracy, yet is told to give land to a foe of the United States: Arab Palestinians in a Two State Solution. In Asia, the State of Taiwan is a long-time friend of the United States and a democracy, yet is told that because of the United States "One China policy" Taiwan has no right to exist as a nation: "There is One China; the People's Republic of China, and Taiwan is part of China." Friends of the United States have to pay the price—in one case by the U.S. policy of a Two State Solution and in the other case by the U.S. policy of a One State Solution.

CHAPTER NINE

MOST OFTEN REPORTED AND TAUGHT: (1975-Forward) "THE CHURCH COMMITTEE TOLD THE TRUTH ABOUT U.S. INTELLIGENCE AGENCIES"

THE TRUTH:

IT DID AND, THEREFORE, TOLD OUR ENEMIES WHAT RUINED OUR INTELLIGENCE FOR DECADES TO COME

After the horror of 9-11 we soon became armed with reports of governmental committees that purported to identify how our intelligence failed us and enabled 9-11 to take place. Among the reports were the most prominent 858 page Joint House and Senate Congressional Report and the 567 page 9-11 Commission Report. All told, the reports gave some 162 conclusions and recommendations.

Many of those who authored the reports attempted to "connect the dots" created during the years of the Clinton and G. W.

Bush Administrations. Those reports made one unforgivable error: they deleted the most significant dots; the ones that were created before those two administrations began, with some of the authors of the reports having been the creators of those dots.

The first dot should have been recorded as the steps taken by the 93rd Congress to remove the foreign policy authority of the President, transferring it to the Congress through continually attaching riders to funding bills to "end the war" in Vietnam, culminating in the War Powers Act. Another dot was the reaction to Watergate that within months of President Nixon's resignation brought about the tremendous majority achieved by the incoming 94th Congress. Even before its final betrayal of the Paris Peace Accords, there was another dot that would lead to 9-11:

Almost as soon as the 94th Congress convened, it assembled a number of congressional committees to investigate U.S. intelligence agencies: the Rockefeller Commission; the House Select Intelligence Committee [known as the Nedzi Committee and became the Pike Committee] and most prominent was the Senate-Select Committee to Study Government Operations with Respect to Intelligence Activities with Senator Frank Church of Idaho as its Chairman. That committee became known as the Senate-Select Committee on Intelligence or the Church Committee.

Prior to then, the Central Intelligence Agency was recognized world-wide as one of the three great international intelligence agencies of the free-world along with MI-6 of Great Britain and Mossad of Israel.

If someone wanted to phone the C.I.A. they would not find it listed in any phone book. If someone wanted to see it they would find no identifying sign along the George Washington Parkway for the correct turn-off to the facility. Those who worked in senior positions of other departments, agencies, and bureaus in Washington,

D.C. were not to refer to it by name but only as 'our friends across the river' to remind the speaker that before saying anything that might be classified, he or she should first be sure of the security clearances and need-to-know of those in attendance. The budget of the C.I.A. was held so secret that only very limited members of the Congress knew its total. It operated largely on what was called a 'black budget' which was supplied by the departments, agencies and bureaus of government contributing a designated amount of their own budgets to the C.I.A. but identified with false headings, without its officers knowing what other departments, agencies, and bureaus were contributing.

Much of the secretiveness was condemned by the 94th Congress' Senate-Select Committee on Intelligence. In addition it recommended that C.I.A. agents no longer deal with 'dirty' foreign groups that our intelligence had always deemed necessary to infiltrate, nor should one U.S. intelligence agency connect with other U.S. agencies on individual cases that could blur the distinction between foreign and domestic spying. The committee also composed a list of those activities from which our intelligence agencies should disengage. Worst of all, on February the 27th of 1975, Senator Church announced that the secrecy oath signed by all C.I.A. employees would be waived, and C.I.A. agents should testify to his committee about those things they had previously sworn to hold secret. C.I.A. Director William Colby agreed.

Some of the finest agents remained silent. After all, they couldn't or wouldn't break their word given in a previously made oath. Other conscientious agents justifiably took early retirement rather than testify. Some simply resigned. But some agents did testify. Revelations then spread around the world aided by dissatisfied dissidents and defectors who had once been with the Agency.

In one country after another, previously held secrets were

printed in anti-U.S. magazines. There were revelations printed in *Liberacion* magazine and Anti magazine, and Counterspy magazine. A magazine called *Covert Action Information Bulletin* exposed over 1,000 names of C.I.A. agents and foreign informants. Richard Welch, U.S. Station Chief in Athens (our C.I.A. agent there) was assassinated by three masked gunmen on December the 23rd of that year, (1975) on his way home from a Christmas party after his name was revealed. He was 46 years old. President Ford neither confirmed nor denied Richard Welch was part of the C.I.A., but there was little public doubt that he was with the C.I.A. as President Ford allowed the burial of Richard Welch at Arlington National Cemetery although Richard Welch would not have been eligible for burial at Arlington since he had not served in the U.S. Armed Forces or qualify under any ordinary exceptions to that requirement.

Because of revelations, it soon became near-impossible to keep or find citizens of foreign countries to help the C.I.A.

Foreign informants declined by 93%.

Those who dropped their affiliation felt if they continued to serve the C.I.A., the jeopardy under which they served would be too much of a risk to their families and to themselves. They faced the possibility of disclosures from the very nation to whom they had given so much. Ours.

Howard Simmons, the Managing Editor of the *Washington Post* had said in reference to the C.I.A. Director: "It's his job to keep secrets. That's his job. My job is to find them." Dan Rather of CBS had said, "My job is to publish and be damned." Lyle Denniston, a reporter for the *Baltimore Sun* had said, "It isn't a question of justification in terms of law. It's a question of justifying it in terms of the commercial sale of information to interested customers. That's my only business. That's the only thing I do in life is to sell information, hopefully for a profit."

During the April 10th, 1975 speech that President Ford gave to a Joint Session of the 94th Congress regarding funds for Vietnam and Cambodia, President Ford also said, "Let me speak quite frankly to some in this Chamber and perhaps to some not in this Chamber. The Central Intelligence Agency has been of maximum importance to Presidents before me. The Central Intelligence Agency has been of maximum importance to me. The Central Intelligence Agency and its associated intelligence organizations could be of maximum importance to some of you in this audience who might be President at some later date. I think it would be catastrophic for the Congress or anyone else to destroy the usefulness by dismantling, in effect, our intelligence systems upon which we rest so heavily."

But, just like his plea for aid to South Vietnam and Cambodia, his plea on retaining our intelligence capabilities was disregarded by the 94th Congress. Those intelligence capabilities were ruined and their ruination caused one intelligence failure after another.

That preceding generation of foreign C.I.A. informants advised their sons and daughters and young friends to work only for those governments that were known to hold confidence, and not to work for any government that was known to have betrayed confidence.

Betrayal in national security and foreign policy became common. When Jimmy Carter became President he took his cue from the State Department and from the success of recent Congresses. His Administration betrayed one foreign friend of the United States after another: President Romero of El Salvador, resulting in a war with the Marxist Guerrillas of the F.M.L.N. [Farabundo Marti Liberation (Front) National]; President Somoza of Nicaragua, resulting in the success of the Sandinistas takeover; transferring diplomatic relations from Taiwan to the People's Republic of China; and betraying the Shah of Iran, an act that ushered in the Ayatollah Khomeini. It was well known within our government that the Ayatollah Khomeini was waiting in Paris for the Shah to leave. Khomeini's wait was over on February 1, 1979. He quickly took the reins of Iran's government. The Carter White House and the State Department were in glee as though Khomeini would be a savior. Our U.S. Ambassador to the United Nations, Andrew Young, stated "Khomeini will be somewhat of a Saint when we get over the panic." Iran then became the first Fundamentalist Revolutionary Islamist Government with terrorism as its backbone. That provided others in neighboring countries to raise a facsimile of his baton. There were a number of Arab leaders who did not want a Persian to be the idol of Islam. They wanted that title.

The two ingredients of February 27, 1975 (the waiving of the secrecy oath) and February 1, 1979 (the Iranian revolution with its birth of a radical Islamist terrorist government) were stirred together. There is an old and wise Arab expression: "It is written." And it was written that it was only a matter of time before the steaming cauldron of those two ingredients would result in tragedies for the peoples of the United States and peoples of other nations around the world.

And so the world was destined to change for the worst.

A nation's survival is most often dependent on intelligence-gathering, and intelligence-gathering is like a giant mosaic painting that is made of thousands and thousands of jig-saw-puzzle-like pieces. You have to find them and put them in place piece by piece.

At a time of war you can't allow any piece to be missing or to fall or to be removed.

Long after the committee hearings and through decades all the way to 9-11 and beyond, the United States had to employ a coalition of intelligence from other nations who did not have a reputation of public exposure.

To trace the connection of the dots did not require commissions, since few if any commission members wanted to revisit the history of the Church Committee. They hoped the Church Committee would be long forgotten. In truth, the destination of the path of dots could have been known and revealed by anyone with a memory of D.C. in 1975.

CHAPTER TEN

MOST OFTEN REPORTED AND TAUGHT: (Years Including Current) "IT IS UNCONSTITUTIONAL FOR THE PRESIDENT TO KEEP NATIONAL SECURITY SECRETS FROM THE CONGRESS"

THE TRUTH:

THE SUPREME COURT WROTE DIFFERENTLY

The most pertinent excerpts follow from the decision of United States v. Curtiss-Wright Export Corporation in which the "external realm" and "external relations" are terms used at times for what is now more frequently called foreign affairs, foreign relations, or foreign policy:

"In this vast external realm, with its important, complicated, delicate and manifold problems, the President alone has the power to speak or listen as a representative of the nation. He makes treaties with the advice and consent of the Senate; but he alone negotiates. Into the field of negotiation the Senate cannot intrude; and

Congress itself is powerless to invade it. As [U.S. Congressman, later to become U.S. Secretary of State and Chief Justice of the U.S. Supreme Court, John] Marshall said in his great argument of March 7, 1800, in the House of Representatives, 'The President is the sole organ of the nation in its external relations, and its sole representative with foreign nations'...The Senate Committee on Foreign Relations at a very early day in our history [February 15, 1816], reported to the Senate, among other things, as follows:

"The President is the constitutional representative of the United States with regard to foreign nations. He manages our concerns with foreign nations and must necessarily be most competent to determine when, how, and upon what subjects negotiation may be urged with the greatest prospect of success. For his conduct he is responsible to the Constitution. The committee consider(s) this responsibility the surest pledge for the faithful discharge of his duty. They think the interference of the Senate in the direction of foreign negotiations calculated to diminish that responsibility, and thereby to impair the best security for the national safety. The nature of transactions with foreign nations, moreover, requires caution and unity of design, and their success frequently depends on secrecy and dispatch.

"It is important to bear in mind that we are here dealing not alone with an authority vested in the President by an exertion of legislative power, but with such an authority plus the very delicate, plenary and exclusive power of the President as the sole organ of the federal government in the field of international relations—a power which does not require as a basis for its exercise an act of Congress, but which, of course, like every other governmental power, must be exercised in subordination to the applicable provisions of the Constitution. It is quite apparent that if, in the maintenance of our international relations, embarrassment—perhaps serious embarrassment—is to be avoided and success for our aims achieved, congressional legislation which is to be made effective through negotiation and inquiry within the international field must often accord to the President a degree of discretion and freedom from statutory restriction which would not be admissible were domestic affairs alone involved. Moreover, he, not Congress, has the better opportunity of knowing the conditions which prevail in foreign countries, and especially is this true in time of war. He has his confidential sources of information. He has his agents in the form of diplomatic, consular and other officials. Secrecy in respect of information gathered by them may be highly necessary, and the premature disclosure of it productive of harmful results. Indeed, so clearly is this true that the First President refused to accede to a request to lay before the House of Representatives the instructions, correspondence and documents relating to the negotiation of the Jay Treaty—a refusal the wisdom of which was recognized by the House itself and has never since been doubted...

"When the President is to be authorized by legislation to act in respect of a matter intended to affect a situation in foreign territory, the legislator properly bears in mind the important consideration that the form of the President's action—or, indeed, whether he shall act at all—may well depend, among other things, upon the nature of the confidential information which he has or may thereafter receive, or upon the effect which his action may have upon our foreign relations. This consideration, in connection with what we have already said on the subject, discloses the unwisdom of requiring Congress in this field of governmental power to lay down narrowly definite standards by which the President is to be governed."

CHAPTER ELEVEN

MOST OFTEN REPORTED AND TAUGHT: (1973 Forward) "THE WAR POWERS ACT PROHIBITS A U.S. PRESIDENT FROM ORDERING MILITARY INTERVENTION WITHOUT CONGRESSIONAL APPROVAL"

THE TRUTH:

IT WOULD HAVE PROHIBITED THAT IF THE U.S. SUPREME COURT HAD NOT ACTED REGARDING CONSTITUTIONALITY IN BOTH 1936 and 1983

There were Schools of Law professors at prominent U.S. east-coast universities who quickly mastered the art of erasure during the years of the theaters of the Cold War. At that time, lists of major U.S. Supreme Court decisions had often included what has been discussed in the previous chapter: United States v. Curtiss-Wright Export Corporation dealing with the powers of the president versus the powers of the congress over the issue of foreign policy, and it had been decided in a way that knocked many political advocacies of law professors for a loop.

That U.S. Supreme Court's decision was made in 1936, so surely at the time of U.S. combat in Southeast Asian battlefields, it had to be considered settled law. Plenty of time had passed for it to be overturned. This left two solutions to the problem of those law professors: erase United States v. Curtiss-Wright Export Corporation from their syllabus or, if a student knew about it and brought it up, argue that the majority decision did not mean what it said—even though there was only one dissenting Justice: James Clark McReynolds. [The majority decision was written by Associate Justice George Sutherland, supported by Chief Justice Charles E. Hughes and five other Justices for a total of seven in the majority. Justice Harlan Fiske Stone did not participate.]

The number of members of the Congresses during the Vietnam-Laos-Cambodia military engagements who even heard of that Supreme Court decision was undoubtedly small and most of that small number surely appreciated its mysterious disappearance from public awareness. [The Curtiss-Wright Export Corporation had been indicted for sending arms to Bolivia against an embargo ordered by President Franklin Delano Roosevelt. Curtiss-Wright's defense was that such an embargo could not be a decision of the President, but should be a congressional order. Curtiss-Wright lost. The Presidency won.] Five Presidents later there came the 1973 debate in the Congress over the War Powers Resolution, transferring major executive authority in foreign affairs to the Congress.

One of the provisions of the War Powers Resolution established that the President in every possible instance should consult with Congress before introducing United States Armed Forces into hostilities, or into situations where imminent involvement in hostilities was clearly indicated by the circumstances, and after every such introduction the President should consult regularly with the Congress until United States Armed Forces would no longer be engaged.

Unfortunately, it didn't stop there: If, within 48 hours after consultation with the Congress, there would be agreement to go ahead and station the troops, the President would have to withdraw them within 60 days unless the Congress extended the 60 day period. And it stated that the President would be able to extend the time an additional 30 days, but only if the President would certify in writing that those 30 days would be necessary to protect U.S. forces during their withdrawal.

It got worse: not only would the President have to get the troops out of imminent hostilities by action of the Congress—but by its inaction: If the Congress would decide to do nothing, our troops would have to leave an area of imminent hostilities in 60 to 90 days. Even during that 60 to 90 day period, the Resolution stated that if the Congress should want an immediate withdrawal of U.S. forces they need only pass a concurrent resolution to that effect which would not be subject to a Presidential veto.

The War Powers congressional passage was only a resolution rather than a law and so it did not have the authority of a law. That was coming. It soon became a bill that passed the Congress. But this bill, like all bills before it, was sent to the White House for the President's signature or his veto. President Nixon vetoed it, calling the bill "both unconstitutional and dangerous to the best interests of the United States." He said, "If this resolution had been in operation, America's effective response to a variety of challenges in recent years would have been vastly complicated or even made impossible. We may well have been unable to respond in the way we did during the Berlin crisis of 1961, the Cuban missile crisis of 1962, the Congo rescue operation in 1964, and the Jordanian crisis of 1970, to mention just a few examples. In addition, our recent actions to bring about a peaceful settlement of the hostilities in the Middle East [our response in the Yom Kippur War] would have been seriously impaired if this resolution had been in force."

The 93rd Congress overrode the President's veto, and the War Powers Resolution that had now become a bill, became the War Powers Act and became a weight on the shoulder of a number of Presidents. Since it has become law, the very threat of Congress invoking the Act has brought about casualties:

It was discovered by the Cable News Network in February, 1982 that a U.S. soldier in El Salvador, Lt. Colonel Harry Melander, was carrying an automatic rifle while he was helping Salvadoran officers replace a bridge that had been destroyed by guerrillas. Orders then came from Washington for Melander to be taken out of El Salvador, and he was reprimanded for having that loaded rifle with him while he helped replace the bridge in dangerous territory; the expulsion and the reprimand consistent with the terms of the War Powers Act. The loaded rifle indicated "imminent hostilities."

A truck came smashing into U.S. Marine Headquarters in Beirut with a cargo of explosives on October 23, 1983, destined to kill 241 U.S. Armed Forces. It rammed through a barbed wire fence and passed through two sentry posts. At both sentry posts, the Marines on duty were armed with unloaded weapons and the Marine guards stated that the truck was going too fast for them to load the bullet clips into their automatic rifles and then fire at the truck. They didn't have bullet-clips already fastened to their rifles because they were obeying orders given consistent with the terms of the War Powers Act. Clips would indicate "imminent hostilities."

When our ships at sea fired at Syrian-held positions that were blasting Beirut, Lebanon, on February 7, 1984, our commanders were ordered to stop, consistent with the terms of the War Powers

Act. Syrian President Hafez al-Assad then knew his victory was assured. Although the U.S. Congress had extended the President's deadline to 18 months under the War Powers Act, there was an announced deadline. President Assad could wait for that deadline to come while the Reagan Administration would be unable to fire on Assad's forces or his allies unless it was a direct act of self-protection. It was not President Assad that stopped the United States when we bombarded Syrian-held positions; it was the threat of Congress' abridgment of the 18 month timetable. The Administration backed off because of a possible indication of "imminent hostilities."

If our military should act beyond self-defense, suggesting that U.S. forces are in an area of imminent hostility without a declaration of war, then the President of the United States is in jeopardy of being in violation of the War Powers Act. If obeyed, the War Powers Act is nothing less than an announcement to the world that the President's word can be overridden by a published timetable that assures our departure from the scene. Even if the War Powers Act is not invoked, an adversary knows that by killing Americans, some members of the Congress may rush to put the Act into effect. Out-waiting the United States can then become a winning procedure anywhere in the world in which our forces are engaged.

Not one President [1973-Current] since it became law has believed it to be constitutional. [Nixon, Ford, Carter, Reagan, Bush 41, Clinton, Bush 43, Obama.] None of them wanted to give it credibility, and at the same time none wanted to blatantly act against it, so they took care not to state they were acting "in compliance with" or acting "under its terms" but rather they were simply acting "consistent with its terms" or "took note of." If their military action ordered was short enough, their report to the Congress came after the completion of the intervention.

President Reagan said, "I would like to emphasize my view that the imposition of such authority and inflexible deadlines creates unwise limitations on Presidential authority to deploy U.S. forces in the interests of U.S. national security. For example, such deadlines can undermine foreign policy judgments, adversely affect our ability to deploy U.S. Armed Forces in support of those judgments, and encourage hostile elements to maximize U.S. casualties in connection with such deployments."

In a court case ten years after the passage of the War Powers Act [on June 23, 1983,] but separate and apart from the War Powers Act, the Supreme Court determined that a House of the Congress cannot impose a legislative veto (as does the War Powers Act) as such a veto would be unconstitutional. The case was Immigration and Naturalization Service v. Chadha. The majority opinion was seven to two, with one of the seven majority opinions being concurrent, meaning in agreement for other or added reasons. It was widely accepted this majority opinion would mean the War Powers Act (filled with congressional action over Presidential decisions) would automatically be unconstitutional although that was not the purpose of the Immigration and Naturalization Service v. Chadha.

With that judgment of the Supreme Court it seemed that the War Powers Act would likely go silently away, but it didn't.

It came up from one Congress to another, most noteworthy being the attempt by 110 members of the 100th Congress bringing President Reagan's 1987 naval operations in the Persian Gulf to the courts. But the Federal Court District Judge tossed it out saying it was a political question and the courts shouldn't be called to resolve such issues. That still wasn't the end of it. President Clinton sent troops to Somalia [1993], Haiti [1994], and Bosnia [1995], all of which were challenged by some members of the Congress. The challenges never went anywhere. Then 31 bipartisan members of the 106th Congress tried to invoke the War Powers Act as reason to deny President Clinton the right to use military intervention in Kosovo [1999] and they brought the case through the lower courts. They lost the case and ultimately the losing members of the Congress brought it to the Supreme Court where the case was refused to be heard. [2000]. As recorded earlier, with little exception in only the rarest of urgent cases, the Supreme Court avoids making political decisions in disputes between the other two branches of government. Most important of all reasons rested in the settled law of the United States v. Curtiss Wright Export Corporation decision of 1936.

After the failure of the congressional attempt regarding Kosovo, the invocation of the War Powers Act has become less and less of a threat as more and more members of forthcoming Congresses recognized that a legislative veto is unconstitutional, and those who didn't recognize that at least knew that if those attempting to invoke the War Powers Act had to go all the way to the Supreme Court, it was unlikely to be considered. Moreover, if the Supreme Court did agree to consider their case, the Court would affirm the Executive Branch's authority since, in order to agree on legislative authority, the Court would be forced to override the long-standing United States v. Curtiss-Wright Export Corporation Supreme Court decision that confirmed the authority of the President in issues of foreign affairs.

That does not, however, change the fact that the War Powers Act is still on the books and can come back to haunt a president in the future. Despite the fact that over seven decades have passed (at this writing) since the U.S. Supreme Court's decision of United States v. Curtiss-Wright Export Corporation, there have been some members of every congress since the 1970s who have been convinced they are in a legislative body in which each member takes part in controlling the movements of the Armed Services, although none of them were elected to fill that position.

That illusion is likely to last a while longer.

CHAPTER TWELVE

MOST OFTEN REPORTED AND TAUGHT: "DISGRACE" (1974 Forward)

THE TRUTH: EXCEPTIONAL

No one—no President—no world leader—no person could compete with the genius of the 37th U.S. President's vision of the world. It was an unexcelled ability, not just to see the world as a globe with close to 200 nations; anyone can do that, but a globe with close to 200 world leaders, all of whom he studied and many of whom he knew.

President Nixon knew their eccentricities, their characters, their friends, their enemies, their fears and their ambitions. And each day would bring about changes in one or more of them with each one having an effect on another. He saw the world as that constantly changing globe, and he kept up with each change and what it could mean to the United States. What he memorized on Saturday had to be revised in his head on Sunday.

During President Nixon's post-presidential years, President Bill Clinton said that Former President Nixon gave him a 1993 report on Russia and President Clinton called that report "The most brilliant communication on foreign policy" that reached him as President.

Judge (and nominee of President Reagan for Associate Justice of the United States Supreme Court) Robert Bork said of President Nixon, "Probably the most intelligent President of (the second) half of the 20th Century."

Senator (and Senate Majority Leader and 1996 Presidential nominee) Bob Dole said that "I believe the second half of the 20th Century will be known as the age of Nixon."

If, during those days, you had your choice between an around-the-world airline ticket or taking a single trip to D.C. or San Clemente or New Jersey or wherever President Nixon may have been at the time, you would have been wise to have turned back the around-the-world ticket in favor of visiting with President Nixon wherever he might have been. That is not in any way to minimize the value of travelling around the world; instead it is that you would have learned much more about the world taking the other course.

Instead of seeing Red Square with its Lenin Mausoleum in Moscow, [with or without the adjoining corpse of Stalin depending on whether it was before or after the end of October, 1961,] you would hear about Nikita Khrushchev who was the leader of the Soviet Union while Nixon was Eisenhower's Vice President, and about Leonid Brezhnev who was the leader of the Soviet Union while Nixon was President of the United States and how Khrushchev was a confrontationalist and seemed unaware of how the United States worked and, in fact, unaware of how so much of the world worked. Brezhnev, however, you would be told, was sharp in his knowledge of the U.S. and the rest of the world, and although strong, saved confrontation only as a last resort. Then President Nixon would tell details; he always knew details. He would say that Brezhnev wore cuff-links while Khrushchev hadn't worn them. He continually absorbed the largest scope of the world combined with the smallest of details. And when put together, all of that gave an important total that was unduplicated by any other participant in world affairs.

Within international events, he could be absorbed by a series of tribal battles in the African country of Upper Volta, and the risk of the tribal battles spreading beyond its borders to Dahomey (receiving little if any stories in the U.S. press or other media) with him continuing, "And Dahomey has enough tribal problems of its own, you know, disrupting their oil production and from there to Nigeria and that's a top oil producer; top oil source, an OPEC country you know since '71, and Europe counts on it. We do, too—to a lesser extent but we do, too—but particularly with European allies dependent on it, you have to think of what that could mean on both sides of the Atlantic—to NATO."

That ability of his was well known by most of those in D.C.; even by those who politically opposed him before his Presidency began, during his Presidency, and after his Presidency.

Then there was the military's view of President Nixon that can be summed up by Colonel Bud Day, a much tortured prisoner of war under the North Vietnamese and was given the Medal of Honor by President Ford. Colonel Day later said: "I was deeply humbled by the Medal of Honor that was given to me by President Ford, but I knew that without President Nixon's conviction and courage, I would have never survived the Hanoi Hilton. It is for this reason that after the White House ceremony with President Ford, I made a special trip to see Former President Nixon in San Clemente for him to ceremonially give me the Medal of Honor."

That kind of statement is still common among those who had been captured and other U.S. Veterans of the Armed Forces who served during those years.

Yet some U.S. historians, to this day, have made careers out of their hatred of him with accent on the Watergate scandal ignoring that Presidents from FDR forward to other pre-Nixon politicians were excluded from having non-policy stories revealed to the public when those stories could be perceived by some as being negative. In this case, "It's the cover-up" has been a chief charge.

There was, indeed, a cover-up; a cover-up of the practice of politics during years and years prior to the Nixon presidency. Not a whisper. No revelations by television or radio personalities or the press. Among those things covered up included the fact that recordings in the White House were made by Presidents from FDR forward. That cover-up allowed the nation to believe that recordings in the White House were the province of President Nixon alone and all of his recordings should therefore be singularly revealed. At the time, no revelations had ever been made of FDR, Truman, Eisenhower, Kennedy, and Johnson. Tapes included many of President Kennedy's and Johnson's telephone calls without the other party knowing they were being recorded. [I find nothing wrong with that and were obviously meant for legitimate purposes both legal and historical.] None of those Presidents were still living to reveal the recordings when President Nixon's tapes were revealed and they would have likely come to his aid had they been living. We do know that those on the staffs who were aware of their President's recordings, remained mute. [The recordings were made on the technology of the times of those Presidents: wax, plastic, 35mm optical tracks, wire recorders, dictabelts, and magnetic tapes.] It took many years for some of their recordings to be brought out to the public and not indiscriminately but with selectivity of family and staffs and Presidential Libraries and Foundations, long after the singular damage had been done to President Nixon. [Again, I find it is correct that they have been brought out by selectivity of family, staffs, and Presidential Libraries and Foundations but that selectivity should have been the same for President Nixon as well as other Presidents.]

Two living, distinguished opponents at that time were Pat Brown who had run and won against him in the race for Governor of California in 1962, and Hubert Humphrey, who had run against him and lost the Presidency to him in 1968. Both of those former opponents said not one word against him during the period that became known as "Watergate." They not only liked him too much to do that but both were very much aware that President Nixon and/or his staff did what had been considered acceptable and done by many politicians and their staffs and went unrevealed by a tight-lipped press long before his Presidency.

The following are some of the most pertinent remarks President Nixon said [on Wednesday, August the 7th, 1974] the day before he announced he would resign: [The quotes were written down later so they may not be precise, but they are as close to their accuracy as possible.]

"Don't ever attack a former President to defend me. Don't do that...

"Lady Bird Johnson is alive, and she's—" and he hunted for words. "—she's a lovely woman. I don't want her to be hurt. Nor Mrs. Kennedy. She's been through hell...

"Our predecessors did good jobs. Even the ones we fought against...Enough good people have been hurt in all this.

"It's my instinct to fight and not quit. I'd fall on the sword. That's my instinct. But let me tell you the way it is. Later on this afternoon a delegation's coming here. Congressional delegation, you know. They're going to give me the count in the House and the Senate. Goldwater, Scott and Rhodes." He extended his arms with the palms of his hands facing the floor, and he gave a swift wave downwards. "I know what they'll say. I know the count. And then tomorrow another delegation...I'll write my book in jail. I don't even mind that. [President of Egypt, Anwar] Sadat said there were eight months of his prison term that was the happiest period of his life. I asked him about that—two months ago when I was in Egypt—I asked him why. He said it was the solitude. You see? The happiest period of his life. He said that he doesn't hold the presidency to be of greater value than himself. Anwar was Anwar whether in jail or in the President's office. It's not the public's acclaim. It's what you know you are...

"So I can write a book in prison if that's what it is. It doesn't make any difference. It doesn't make any difference. I can do that. I didn't remember what I said when—you know I talk—or what it would sound like on tape years later, separate from everything else. They'll drain these things out little by little. Every time I think it's over, there are more things in those tapes that they'll make something out of. Then we'll continue to be on the defensive. And you can't do anything when you're just defending and trying to remember what you meant when you said something years ago, and weren't even paying any attention to what it would sound like if someone wanted to make something of it. So you can count on it. There will be more and more. It will just go on. It's time to stop this agony from becoming the nation's daily exercise. That's what it will become if I stay... (But then I won't be President, so it won't make any difference to the country.) It's better that I let them destroy me rather than bring about the destruction of our foreign policy—the destruction of the Presidency...And it could bring down our institutions.

"Can you imagine our country's place in the world if they bring down our ability to gather intelligence? They wouldn't stop. Look what they've done already. The press isn't composed of Horace Greeleys anymore, you know. I have a choice right now to make it worse for me or make it worse for the whole country.

"Whether I'm in the White House or out of it, there may be no way out for Vietnam with this Congress or the next one. They don't want to save the Vietnamese. But they may be more sensible if I leave. If I fight it out, foreign policy will be in shambles. This thing can go on and on and Brezhnev can take advantage of it. Why not? Why shouldn't he? I would if I were him. Brezhnev will know that the President of the United States is in a weakened position, a President without teeth. It's likely that he'll take advantage of it. He wouldn't be a leader if he didn't. He's likely to mount another crisis in the Mideast. Look what happened last October when I called the alert. They thought—the press thought—they thought I did it to divert attention from Watergate. Everything I need to do will be suspect. As President I won't be able to do anything. You see, I can't govern and he'll know it. No one will be governing. They won't let me do anything. They'll stop everything. If I stay, you have to realize all three branches of the government will be wrapped up in this thing—and not just for three or four months. It could go on for two years. All three branches paralyzed by this. If I was Brezhnev and saw this weakness going on and on—no, no, no. And I'm the only one who can end it—quickly, and be done with it. And they'll have Jerry Ford."

That was Wednesday. He announced his resignation on Thursday night and he left the White House on Friday.

It was one night the following week on Washington D.C.'s *Ten O'clock Evening News* of Metromedia, Channel 5; when someone-on-camera used the expression, “resigned in disgrace.” It became the expression picked up by media throughout the country and is still used by fools at worst, and the misinformed at best. “Disgrace” was not the appropriate word. “Exceptional” was appropriate and so was “thoughtful of others including those he had politically opposed” and so was “the United States as his first interest” and so was “the importance of U.S. Allies, particularly South Vietnam” and so was “not giving Leonid Brezhnev of the Soviet Union the opportunity to take advantage of the then current circumstances in the capital city of the United States.”

If only everyone was that disgraceful.

CHAPTER THIRTEEN

MOST OFTEN REPORTED AND TAUGHT: (Many Years Including Current) "THE U.S. GOVERNMENT GIVES THE PEOPLE THEIR UNALIENABLE RIGHTS"

THE TRUTH:

THE DECLARATION OF INDEPENDENCE IS CLEAR THAT THE ENDOWMENT OF CERTAIN UNALIENABLE RIGHTS DOES NOT COME FROM THE GOVERNMENT BUT FROM THE CREATOR

It has become common to hear someone in political life say that "health care is a right" or "a college education is a right" or "housing is a right." Add to the list any number of things that are hoped to be rights by some while known not to be rights by others. Those items not enumerated in the U.S. Constitution may well be valuable objectives but they are not rights. Nor should anyone look to government to create rights as the rights of the people cannot be given by government and therefore cannot be taken away by government.

It is also important to know that itemized rights do not have to cost any other person involved in financing those rights.

In short, you may worship where you choose, but no one is compelled by government to finance your place of worship.

You may speak as you choose, but no one is compelled by government to pay for your pedestal or auditorium or microphone.

You may print what you choose, but no one is compelled by government to finances its printing or publication.

You may assemble where you choose including for the petitioning of government, but no one is compelled by government to finance your assembly or petition.

The individual cannot expect to demand the payment of others to bring them about as that would take away the right of those others to endorse or discourage as they themselves may choose.

Many dictatorships copied parts of the U.S. Constitution but were careful not to copy our Founders use of government's prohibition from establishing or prohibiting rights. The dictatorships just gave lists of things without a demand they would keep their own hands off:

Article 34 in the Constitution of the former Soviet Union stated: "Citizens of the USSR are equal before the law, without distinction of origin, social or property status, race or nationality, sex, education, language, attitude to religion, type and nature of occupation, domicile, or other status. The equal rights of citizens of the USSR are guaranteed in all fields of economic, political, social, and cultural life." Article 49 stated that "persecution for criticism is prohibited" and Article 50 guaranteed "freedom of speech, of the press, and of assembly, meetings, street processions and demonstrations." None of those written things meant anything since citizens of the Soviet Union learned at early ages that their government was doing those things the government wanted to do at the time they wanted to do them. If there is a right given by the government to the individual the individual knows that the government can take away that right at will.

The People's Republic of China's Constitution gives all kinds of rights by the government: Article 35 of the Constitution of the People's Republic of China states: "Citizens of the People's Republic of China enjoy freedom of speech, of the press, of assembly, of association, of procession and of demonstration." Article 36 guarantees "freedom of religious belief." Article 34 gives the right to vote and stand for election. None of it means anything.

Such constitutions never stated what has been so starkly stated in the First Amendment of the United States Constitution that "Congress shall make no law respecting an establishment of religion, or prohibiting the free exercise thereof; or abridging the freedom of speech, or of the press, or the right of the people peaceably to assemble, and to petition the Government for a redress of grievances." The difference is that this was written to warn government to stay out of the business of the people, not for the people to stay out of the business of government.

Liberia, upon its Founding in 1847, copied the United States Constitution to the point of creating the same three branches of government as the U.S.; a Judiciary and an Executive and a Legislature composed of a Senate of two Senators per county (in their case) and a House of Representatives based on a population census with similarities to the U.S. In addition the capital city was named Monrovia in honor of U.S. President James Monroe and another Liberian city was named after U.S. President James Buchanan. Its flag was designed with great similarities to the flag of the United States, and its currency became the dollar.

Most important, Liberia's Constitution recognized God-given natural rights of the people. Liberia's Constitution was written magnificently and in many areas more detailed than the U.S. Constitution. But in short time parts of it were not obeyed by the Liberian government. That Constitution gives evidence that no matter its writer's careful and complete considerations, their superb writings once accepted, can quickly mean nothing when not obeyed by the government and not able to be demanded by the people.

Within the Constitution of the United States is the Preamble explaining why a government is necessary and gives all credit to "We the People," not "We the Government." That is followed by three Articles explaining the duties of each of the three branches of government, then four more Articles and twenty-seven Amendments, including the first ten which are the Bill of Rights. The entire document takes no more room than a passport.

The Constitution has become this generation's inheritance; a treasure to be used as a guide for ourselves and to be an escort and tutor for the members of our government, no matter their rank.

That is because the Founders of the United States had the wisdom to know the values of liberty, quality, and brevity.

CHAPTER FOURTEEN

MOST OFTEN REPORTED AND TAUGHT: (2010 Forward) "ALL BILLS SHOULD BE READ BY MEMBERS OF THE CONGRESS BEFORE VOTING FOR OR AGAINST THEM"

THE TRUTH: IT WON'T HAPPEN UNTIL ALL BILLS ARE WRITTEN FOR READABILITY

It has happened time and time again; Members of the Congress vote one way or another on passage or non-passage of a bill and later they confess they never read the bill before voting on it.

Most famously, on March the 9th of 2010 Democrat Speaker of the House Nancy Pelosi, while speaking to the 2010 Legislative Conference for the National Association of Counties said "...We have to pass the bill so that you can find out what is in it—away from the fog of the controversy." Her reference was to the Patient Protection and Affordable Care Bill otherwise known as Obama

Care but it could have been for countless bills. Republican Congressman Michael Burgess of Kentucky who opposed the bill was honest enough to say that Pelosi was right in her remark but that "I wouldn't recommend anyone actually broadcasting that."

Any number of members of the Congress agreed with that but most were not public in their silent nods and quick audible change of subjects.

Those who were also members of the Congress in 1993 as well as 2010 had been through this before with public exposure—coincidentally with a health bill: the most prominent first public exposure of a bill's length and non-readability. It was called the Health Security Act even though it wasn't an Act but a bill in the 103rd Congress during President Bill Clinton's Administration with the bill also known as being under the President's wife's purview and often publically called "Hillary Care."

It was a bill of 1,342 pages of incoherent English. The following was selected by a student to prove the point of incoherency by simply opening the book and reading what the chance-opening revealed. This particular excerpt was from Page 205 but could have been from Page Anything. Incoherency is not a rarity but a habit of style among the congressional staffers who bring a bill to completion:

"In the case of a corporate alliance with a sponsor described in section 1311 (b) (1) (A), the sponsor shall provide for the funding of benefits, through insurance or otherwise, consistent with section 6131, the applicable solvency requirements of sections 1395 and 1396, and any rules established by the Secretary of Labor..."

The reader of that bill and countless other bills are often confronted with a need to have hundreds of other documents near so as to read what references are being listed. Of course no Representative or Senator reads all bills in full. Most are unreadable.

In contrast, James Madison wrote very clearly: "It will be of little avail to the people that the laws are made by men of their own choice, if the laws be so voluminous that they cannot be read, or so incoherent that they cannot be understood; if they be repealed or revised before they are promulgated, or undergo such incessant changes that no man who knows what the law is today can guess what it will be tomorrow. Law is defined to be a rule of action; but how can that be a rule which is little known and less fixed?"

One Rule of the Congress (without an Amendment needed) could take note of James Madison's statement by making "any bill submitted shall be no longer than the length of the United States Constitution and written by those members of the Congress who choose to be understood by the populace in the style of writing used for clear comprehension." After all, that pocket-sized document has worked well in defining and explaining the entire system of the United States of America.

CHAPTER FIFTEEN

MOST OFTEN REPORTED AND TAUGHT: (Many Years Including Current) "ALL LAWS MUST REMAIN THE SAME IN WAR AS IN PEACE"

THE TRUTH:

NOT DURING WARS THAT RISK THE SURVIVAL OF THE U.S. OR ITS ALLIES

If you were an American working or visiting Cambodia any time from the beginning of the Southeast Asian Theater of the Cold War through 1974 it would have been normal to believe a Khmer Rouge communist take-over of Cambodia could never happen there. Eating Kellogg's Corn Flakes for breakfast at Le Royal Hotel among international guests and U.S. Military and U.S. Embassy Officers did not present a picture of imminent Khmer Rouge horror of their quickly coming genocide.

But Cambodia surrendered to the Khmer Rouge on April the 17th of 1975 and that horror of genocide became reality.

If during those years through 1974 you were an American working or visiting South Vietnam it would have been normal to believe a North Vietnamese communist take-over of South Vietnam could never happen there. Saigon's Ton Son Nhut Air Base and Airport's massive landing strips and adjoining territory were filled to every horizon with camouflaged U.S. war planes.

But South Vietnam surrendered to the North Vietnamese on April the 30th of 1975 and Re-Education Camps were built and filled with political prisoners and over one-half million South Vietnamese Boat People were estimated to have been drowned and are still under the South China Sea. Most died using aborted pieces of wood hurriedly used as boats in attempted escape from the North Vietnam victors.

If you were an American working or visiting Iran prior to the end of 1978 it would have been normal to believe the rumored revolution of an Ayatollah would never come and the friendly Pro-West government of the Shah was to continue with no real risk. In the Covered Bazaar shopping for gifts to take home, there was not a hint that a jihadist terrorist revolution could be successful.

But the Pro-Jihadist terrorist government won a quick revolution on February the 1st of 1979. In less than a year Iran became the leading terrorist government in the world.

For so many years the U.S. power and will appeared to be too strong to ever allow anything but the ultimate victory of those friendly and allied governments with the United States. And it was common for any American walking the streets of those allied nations during the pre-surrender days of those countries to be hugged by strangers—for one reason—for being an American and attempting their rescue from totalitarians. It was like being in the cavalry in an old black and white Warner Brothers film with a bugler in the lead of countless advancing soldiers on horses and with cheering civilians standing outside of taverns and a blacksmith pausing in his pounding work, lifting his glass of beer to toast the cavalry while his tears of joy drifted from his eyes to his cheeks.

Of course many people were not rescued and not all nations were kept free, and today many believe that even though revolutions and victories of totalitarians occurred elsewhere, at least it can't happen here in the United States. They do not think that the U.S. could lose a war with the U.S. taken by a foreign power. But it can. It can lose as others have lost their wars—unless the U.S. cares enough to recognize that wars for a nation's survival have always called for extraordinary measures to insure that victory is achieved rather than flirting with defeat.

During the Civil War President Lincoln suspended Habeas Corpus. People were sent to prison without charges made, without the length of incarceration known to the prisoner.

During World War One, while Woodrow Wilson was President, imprisonment was imposed on many writers and publishers publically opposed to the U.S. being involved in the war, including conscientious objectors, some of whom were later reported to have been sent to Alcatraz.

During World War Two President Franklin Delano Roosevelt directed and signed Executive Order 9066 which brought about internment in Relocation Camps for over 100,000 of those with Japanese ancestry including a massive majority of U.S. citizens. For the non-military of the nation under FDR there was a requirement beyond cash: For most purchases it was necessary to have the appropriate coupons and different colored chips and there were stickers for windshields with the letters A or B or C on them to designate how much gasoline could be purchased. There was rationing of shoes, butter, meat, sugar, and anything made of metal or rubber. Almost every commodity was being rationed or was not available at all.

But after those wars of survival were over, the freedoms suspended during those wars were not only restored but greatly enhanced:

After the Civil War came Amendments 13, 14, and 15 to the U.S. Constitution guaranteeing the end of slavery.

After World War One came the 19th Amendment guaranteeing women's suffrage; the right of an equal vote for women as had by men.

After World War Two came integration of the U.S. Armed Forces and the integration of the federal bureaucracy paving the way for court decisions of the 1950s and the Civil Rights Law of 1964 and the Voting Rights Law of 1965.

Even before those wars, there were stories that during the U.S. Revolutionary War atrocities were committed by both sides. Maybe. What we do know is that after that war came the U.S. Constitution with its Bill of Rights.

And even after all those wars, during the 46 years of the Cold War fought under President Truman through George H.W. Bush during nine presidencies, saw what would be called by some as excessive presidential powers—possibly illegal if used during peace-time.

We simply forget that the wars for national survival that this nation won had, at times, called for extraordinary measures to insure we would achieve victory rather than increase the risk of defeat. Presidents felt the greatest risk was to the very survival of the United States, as the nation was engaged in fighting against strong foreign enemies.

Today polls indicate that a majority of Americans complain of being war-weary since 2001. No they aren't. Other than ones who have served or are still serving, or who has another they love who has served or is still serving, most Americans do not regularly wake up thinking of what they can do for the war effort and they don't regularly go to bed wondering what they can do tomorrow for the war effort. The term "war-effort" is not even in the average American's vocabulary.

Now we are engaged in a World War against Radical Islamist Jihadists. At this writing in 2015 we are losing in Syria, Iraq, Yemen, Libya, Sinai, Gaza, Nigeria, Cameroon, Mali, Chad, Somalia, Afghanistan, Pakistan, Iran; all those nations being under hostile governments or attack by those Radical Islamist Jihadists who have their eyes and weapons on Algeria, Tunisia, Turkey, Lebanon, Jordan, Israel, and all the Arab Gulf States. On other fronts in this World War, freedom is losing from expansion by force of Russia; as noted earlier, the Crimea having been invaded and seized by Russia and Eastern Ukraine under current daily and nightly attacks, and in Asia the South China Sea and East China Sea islands are being taken by the government of the People's Republic of China disregarding all international laws of the sea with its claims.

Allies of the People's Republic of China, both Russia and North Korea, are supporting the military of Iran jumping borders of the world. And the U.S. Government is making deals with Cuba, Iran, and North Korea, greatly confusing friends of the United States.

If only this nation could relearn what has been so evident. FDR knew how to fight a war. If a President of the future says that he or she will end the war in which we may be engaged—and do it without victory, what that President means is that the President will lose the war.

That is because wars do not end. Wars are won or lost. That's all there is.

CHAPTER SIXTEEN

MOST OFTEN REPORTED AND TAUGHT: (1983 Forward) "PRESIDENT REAGAN NAMED HIS ANTI-MISSILE DEFENSE PROGRAM, 'STAR WARS'"

THE TRUTH:

NO. SENATOR TED KENNEDY USED THE FILM TITLE IN RIDICULE OF PRESIDENT REAGAN'S STRATEGIC DEFENSE INITIATIVE

The United States could have had a ballistic missile defense by the end of the 1980s, but it was rejected immediately after President Reagan presented his idea based on the "High Frontier" concept of General Daniel Graham. On March 23, 1983, President Reagan, in a nationally televised address, appealed to American scientists to "turn their great talents" to development of an antiballistic missile system capable of destroying launched missiles before they could reach their targets. He said, "I am directing a comprehensive and intensive effort to define a long term research and development program to begin to achieve our ultimate goal of eliminating the threat posed by strategic nuclear missiles." And he asked, "Wouldn't it be better to save lives than to avenge them?"

Senator Ted Kennedy immediately accused the President of using "misleading Red Scare tactics and reckless Star War schemes." That phrase of identification was quickly picked up by the national media.

Dan Rather on the CBS Evening News introduced a CBS reporter by saying, "Pentagon correspondent David Martin has been investigating the President's Star Wars strategy. Tonight his report on dealing death from space at the speed of light." The report started and David Martin said that the President's initiative sounded like the "ultimate death ray" and that it would be "murderously expensive." All the trigger phrases—star wars, death from space, death ray, murderously expensive—were used while not admitting that its purpose was not to kill one living creature but, rather, to destroy a nuclear warhead while already en route to the United States.

The Congress got into it as well:

Senator Mark Hatfield said, "The President's advisors must be called to account for these terrifying proposals."

Senator Alan Cranston called it a "nightmare."

Senator Gary Hart said with sarcasm, "Once upon a time there was an evil empire that threatened us with terrible weapons. But then one day, our side discovered a magic invisible shield. When we stretched it across our country, no missiles could penetrate it. From that day on, we stopped worrying about nuclear war and lived happily after." The audience laughed.

All at once, politicians and the national networks and news magazines and leading newspapers became instruments that adopted Senator Kennedy's phrase of ridicule rather than using the name of the Strategic Defense Initiative (SDI), given to it by the President.

Previously, there had been a tradition for the major media to use the name a President gave to his own initiatives. The major media had used the names; FDR's "The New Deal," Truman's "The Fair Deal," Eisenhower's "Atoms for Peace" and "People to People Programs" and "Open Skies," JFK's "The New Frontier" and "The Alliance for Progress," LBJ's "The War on Poverty" and "The Great Society." But this would be different. In this case, the name given to it by its opposition would be used: "Star Wars."

Therefore, when a reference to the President's initiative appeared in the national media, there was an immediate signal of mockery to the reader or the audience. Even conservatives, thoughtlessly, picked it up.

Ridiculing an idea is the best way to stop it. Ridicule of name, of expense, and of plausibility, became the devices of opposition to the Strategic Defense Initiative.

Contrast this with the reaction to another President's initiative also of great scope and cost and an unworldly objective: On May 25, 1961, President Kennedy called a Joint Session of the Congress. He had already given his State of the Union Address and his calling of the session was unique. He said, "The Constitution imposes upon me the obligation to from time to time give to the Congress information on the state of the union. While this has traditionally been interpreted as an annual affair, this tradition has been broken in extraordinary times. These are extraordinary times." He then went on to propose spending for defense beyond what he had proposed in his original State of the Union Address, but then he added something.

He said, "I believe this nation should commit itself to achieving the goal, before this decade is out, of landing a man on the moon and returning him safely to earth."

The Congress and the nation validated the commitment with

jubilance. Cost? Not known. Could it be done? Nothing like it had been done before. The most we had accomplished at that time was to send Alan Shepherd up in a capsule that fit him like a glove. He had simply gone up and down in that capsule without orbit, and President Kennedy's request for a lunar journey was made only twenty days after the Alan Shepherd fifteen minute non-orbital space flight. Yet we would immediately start preparations to go to the moon.

With press and public support, the deadlines were met and, as President Kennedy wanted for the United States, man was on the moon "before this decade is out." It took great courage for anyone, particularly a President, to say we would do something for which the technology didn't exist, and which would have to be so expensive with an immense amount of inventions to be scheduled starting from nothing more solid than imagination. But that was another President twenty-two years before the request of a Strategic Defense Initiative.

The East Room was filled with the White House Press Corps, and President Reagan was at the podium. The first question of the News Conference was asked by Helen Thomas of United Press International and she referred to President Reagan's initiative twice in her question as "Star Wars," the name given it by Senator Kennedy.

The President said, "Helen, I wish whoever coined that expression would take it back again because it gives a false impression of what it is we're talking about."

He went on to answer her question, and then she said, "Star Wars—even if you don't like the term—" and she went on.

Because so few in political life and in the major media refused to learn the name he had given it; the "Strategic Defense Initiative", in President Reagan's Second Inaugural he referred to his proposal as the "Security Shield," but practically no one used his term no matter what he wanted to call it.

Those in the Congress and those in the media who opposed the President's initiative, immediately had an ally. The ally in rallying against this proposal was the government of the Soviet Union. Soviet Communist Party General Secretary, Yuri Andropov, said, "Engaging in this is not just irresponsible, it is insane."

The Soviet's Chief Negotiator in Geneva, Viktor Karpov, said that any progress in arms talks can be ruled out as long as the United States continues research on its "Star Wars program."

The Soviet Union's Foreign Minister, Eduard Shevardnadze, said to the U.N. General Assembly: "To counter the sinister plan of Star Wars, the USSR is putting before the international community, a concept of Star Peace."

Yuri Andropov again: "All attempts at achieving military superiority over the Soviet Union are futile. The Soviet Union will never allow it to succeed. We will never be caught defenseless by any threat."

Andrei Gromyko gave praise to those who wanted a Nuclear Freeze; not what he called a "Star Wars program." He said that Moscow expresses solidarity with the nuclear freeze movement "because we are of like mind...the movement and the Soviet Union are comrades in the cause to prevent nuclear war."

In August of 1985, *The New York Times* printed a three-quarter page advertisement paid for by the Soviet Embassy in Washington. It was a reprint from an editorial in Pravda headlined, "What Holds Back Progress at the Geneva Talks?" Then the article went on to say that President Reagan was "torpedoing arms control by stubbornly forging ahead with Star Wars."

The USSR issued a glossy fifty-six page pamphlet charging the United States with blackmail through "Star Wars." More than seventy thousand copies were printed in English, Spanish, German, Italian, French, and Japanese.

Director of the Soviet Union's Institute of the United States and Canada, Georgi Arbatov, said of President Reagan's initiative: "We never had it in mind that it's possible to do it. It's a vision. We don't believe it even now. We think it's practically impossible to implement."

The Soviet Union launched a campaign against the President's idea because the Soviet Union saw their massive superiority of ICBM's endangered, should the President's idea succeed. The legacy of Leonid Brezhnev was in peril since the warhead payloads under the nose-cones on top of Soviet missiles might be made impotent. The Soviet Academy of Sciences issued a statement that President Reagan's plan was "both unworkable and costly." But if it was unworkable and costly, instead of opposing it, why wouldn't the members of the Soviet Academy of Sciences have been laughing inside the Kremlin walls in the hope that we would waste as much of our money as possible on it?

The Soviets were, however, so concerned about it working that their negotiators left the Geneva Arms Talks for the sole purpose of influencing President Reagan to abandon his plan for a Strategic Defense Initiative. President Reagan let them leave. They came back.

After they came back, a plan emerged for a Geneva Summit between President Reagan and the new USSR General Secretary, Mikhail Gorbachev.

Former President Jimmy Carter called President Reagan's Strategic Defense Initiative, "the key obstacle to success" at the scheduled Geneva Summit saying that "It is ill conceived, a total waste of money and counterproductive."

The Geneva Summit was well conceived with no waste of money and totally productive from the standpoint of the United

States. The objective of General Secretary Gorbachev was a failure. His objective in Geneva and throughout coming Summits was for President Reagan to give up the Strategic Defense Initiative but President Reagan remained immovable. His repeated immovability gave added power and credibility to his call in Berlin to "Mister Gorbachev—tear down this Wall!"

The policies of President Reagan's intransigence followed into the first year of George H.W. Bush's Presidency when the Berlin Wall was torn down. And that was followed by the end of the Warsaw Pact, the organization of the Soviet Union's satellite nations. And then, in fact, came the end of the Soviet Union itself.

CHAPTER SEVENTEEN

MOST OFTEN REPORTED AND TAUGHT: (2002 Forward) "PRESIDENT GEORGE W. BUSH SHOULD NEVER HAVE ORDERED THE INVASION OF IRAQ"

THE TRUTH:

ANY CONSCIENTIOUS PRESIDENT FROM WORLD WAR TWO FORWARD WOULD HAVE DONE THAT

First, a hypothetical by imagining the following scenario occurred: assume the Director of the C.I.A., George Tenet, came into the Oval Office in July of 2001 and said, "Mr. President, I have very tough news. Based on information from unassailable foreign informants, there will be a massive attack on the United States some two months or so from today. It is being planned by Al Qaeda which is being sheltered by the Taliban Government of Afghanistan. Our operatives have been associating with them. The attack will be directly committed by 19 Islamic fundamentalists, 15 of them here from Saudi Arabia. Our friends at the Bureau have been conducting surveillance on all 19. We know where they are. And I must stress that our people and the foreign informants who confirmed this information are beyond reproach. Totally reliable. We do not know where the attack will take place on our country or how, but the plan is for the attack to be like nothing we've known before, and it is planned to cause a tremendous catastrophe to the United States. That's all we know."

After some questioning and conversation, Director Tenet walks from the Oval Office, leaving the President alone. And the President thinks. And paces. And thinks. And paces. And thinks.

Based on the information he has been given, the President orders preemptive action including the bombing and invasion of Afghanistan to bring about a regime change from Mullah Muhammad Omar of the Taliban Government.

The President is successful and he reduces Al Qaeda to hiding in caves. Moreover, within the United States, the President quickly orders the immediate arrest of the 19 men who were scheduled to perform the attack on the United States, and they are imprisoned in Guantanamo Bay Naval Base.

Then comes September the 11th—and there is no attack. It is a normal Tuesday in the United States: baseball games, preparations continue for the Emmy Awards, ESPN has an interview with tennis champion, Venus Williams, the nightly news has a segment on a flurry of shark attacks, Washington D.C. is talking about the hearings on the appointment of John Negroponte as the U.S. Ambassador to the U.N. An ordinary September day. And most important of all, away from the news, those who walked into New York City's twin towers of the World Trade Center in the morning, walk out of those buildings in the evening. And they go to their homes. And it's a routine day at the Pentagon, and a routine day in Somerset County of Pennsylvania.

The President would most likely have been condemned. "After all," it would have been said, "we suddenly bombed and overthrew the government of a foreign country, even though that government never did anything against the United States, and they had no weapons of mass destruction or even any weapons beyond the most primitive. What could they have possibly used against us? And we imprisoned 19 people. We sent them to Guantanamo without any evidence they did anything."

Although the President's preemptive actions would have saved the lives of some three thousand people and the grief of the countless, his Presidency would probably have been over. Who would have believed that he acted wisely, particularly if he didn't give the sources of intelligence, so as not to jeopardize their safety? And particularly after the findings of the Church Committee some 26 years earlier.

So, of course, that conversation with George Tenet did not take place. None of that happened.

In reality, during the first two weeks after 9-11 it was apparent to the nation that preemptive action would be necessary to avoid such a future catastrophe. That didn't last long. Move the calendar forward, not to another hypothetical scenario, but a real one: Many who served on the commissions that later concluded that President George W. Bush did not "connect the dots" that led to 9-11, without even a blink of hesitancy accused the President of taking preemptive action against Iraq, in which he did connect the dots: the dots of Saddam Hussein's history of terrorism, rape rooms for women; videotaping the throwing of male prisoners from the top of buildings; his public hatred for the United States; the planned but thwarted bombing of Radio Free Europe and Radio Liberty facilities in the Czech Republic; his invasion of Kuwait; our monitoring of no-fly zones for the ten years following our liberation of Kuwait while Saddam Hussein's government tried to shoot our monitoring planes down; the intended assassination of President Bush (41) in Kuwait; his financial rewards to families of Arab-Palestinian suicide bombers; and his use of chemical weapons on Iraqi Shias and Kurds. These were all dots, including warnings of new weapons of mass destruction given to the President by our C.I.A.; by the S.I.S. [MI6], the British Secret Intelligence Service; by the D.G.S.E., the French Directorate-General for External Security; by the B.N.D., the German's Intelligence agency called the Bundesnachrichtendienst; by President Hosni Mubarak of Egypt; by King Abdullah II of Jordan; and even by President Vladimir Putin of Russia. Could any responsible President of the United States have ignored such warnings? Such dots?

The great long-term harm that has been done by the dissent over our preemptive action in Iraq is that preemptive action is now known to be a tremendous domestic risk for a president. It is entirely possible that, knowing the dissenting reactions of many regarding Iraq, a president may not do what must be done for our survival as a nation: take preemptive actions—likely against the government of Iran or North Korea or Syria or Somalia or Yemen or some other menacing state, or by Hezbollah or Hamas. Some president may wait until it's too late rather than suffer domestic political consequences. That, of course, would depend on whether the president would care more about the perception of that president's legacy than the risk of what may well become the future of the nation.

CHAPTER EIGHTEEN

MOST OFTEN REPORTED AND TAUGHT:
(Many Years)
NEGOTIATIONS WITH FRIEND OR FOE ARE VITAL

THE TRUTH:

20TH CENTURY NEGOTIATIONS OF 1938, 1945, 1953, 1961, 1972, 1973, 1980s, 1991, 1993, 1994, and 1995 FAILED

The 20th Century illustrated that attempts to negotiate with tyrannies are useless unless the free nation warns, and is known to mean, that any violation of an agreement will bring about immediate peril for the tyranny.

Negotiations didn't work in 1938 in Munich when the United Kingdom's Prime Minister Neville Chamberlain signed an agreement with Germany's Chancellor Adolph Hitler and proclaimed the agreement gave Great Britain "peace in our time."

Or in 1945 in Yalta when President Roosevelt and Prime Minister Churchill signed the Yalta Agreements with Joseph Stalin of the Soviet Union promising that those countries to come under a Soviet victory would be given democratic governments. Soon they were turned into proxies of the Soviet Union. It took some 46 years to correct that.

Or in 1953 at Panmunjom with North Korea. That was when North Korea was a threat to South Korea alone. Over one-half century later it was a threat to the world. General Mark Clark had written that "In carrying out the instructions of my government I gained the unenviable distinction of being the first United States Army commander in history to sign an armistice without victory."

Or in 1961 between President Kennedy and Chairman Nikita Khrushchev in Vienna over Laos and Berlin. Khrushchev judged him severely and less than three months later built the Berlin Wall, and then put missiles and bombers in Cuba, bringing about the Cuban Missile Crisis of October, 1962.

Or in 1972 when Leonid Brezhnev of the Soviet Union agreed to an Anti-Ballistic Missile Treaty. Among violations the Soviet Union built and deployed a prohibited large phased array radar station near Krasnoyarsk. Many other violations were suspected but were not confirmed until after the Soviet Union became extinct.

Or in 1973 in Paris with North Vietnam signing the Paris Peace Accords in which major provisions of non-aggression were violated by the North Vietnamese, with the paramount violation committed by the United States Congress by disobeying the provision of the Accords that called for appropriate U.S. aid to South Vietnam if there was aggression by the North Vietnamese. The Congress denied that aid causing South Vietnam to surrender to North Vietnam.

Or in 1980 when the United States, through Algeria, made an agreement with Iran including that U.S. hostages could not take legal action against the Government of Iran and that all assets in the U.S. of the late Shah and his relatives must go to the government of

Iran. In addition, among other provisions the United States agreed to revoke all trade sanctions and withdraw all claims against Iran, as well as bar and preclude prosecution against Iran of any pending or future claims of U.S. nationals rising out of the hostage crisis.

Or throughout the 1980s with five Summits held between U.S. President Reagan and Soviet General Secretary Gorbachev. Wisely, no agreement was made by President Reagan in Geneva or Reykjavik or Moscow or Governor's Island. He did, however, make an agreement, proven unwisely, in Washington, D.C. phasing out Intermediate Range Nuclear Forces that brought repeated Soviet violations until the U.S. and Russia (in the 21st Century) both withdrew from the agreement.

Or in 1991 when the government of Iraq agreed with the U.N. to enforce Iraqi No-Fly Zones subject to inspection by coalition aircraft, and then Iraq fired at those inspecting aircraft. [Throughout the 1990s the United Nations passed some sixteen resolutions spelling out violations of Saddam Hussein's government of Iraq, and the U.N. promptly disregarded their own resolutions.]

Or in 1993 when the Oslo Accords were signed on the South Lawn of the White House by Yasser Arafat promising peace in exchange for land. Israel gave land and Arafat, in exchange, gave violent uprisings and terrorism including a later intifada [with this one lasting four years starting in 2004].

Or in 1994 in Pyongyang, North Korea when Former President Jimmy Carter during President Clinton's Administration, went to North Korea and visited Kim il Sung and together they inaugurated the Agreed Framework regarding nuclear weapons in which North Korea confirmed its willingness to freeze its nuclear weapons program for which North Korea would receive escalated aid from the U.S., South Korea, and Japan. Key elements were being implemented when in 2005 North Korea admitted that it had now manufactured nuclear weapons as a "nuclear deterrent for self-defense." On October 9, 2006, North Korea conducted a nuclear test. Further nuclear tests were conducted in 2006 and 2009.

Or in 1995 in Dayton, Ohio when the government of Serbia signed the Dayton Accords to bring an end to further killings in Bosnia. The killings were moved to Kosovo by Slobodan Milosevic of the Serbian Government.

Recognize that the U.S. Department of State has negotiations as its business; its craft; and without much if any exception advises Presidents of the United States to negotiate no matter if the other side is friend or tyrant. There seems to be little interest in the lessons of the 20th Century having been learned going into the 21st Century.

Tyrannical governments that don't care about their own citizens surely do not care about honoring their signature with a foreign government. That signature is not perceived by them as an obligation, but perceived by them as a device to maintain their hold and to expand their territory.

Unlike the value of negotiating with free nations and among most governments with whom disputes arise, an oppressive and expansionist government should not have more than one totally monitored chance to offer the end of an international dispute. Once such a chance fails, unless a free nation can talk with that tyranny about the date, the protocols and the modalities regarding the documents necessary for an unconditional surrender of the tyranny, what are generally called "peace talks" are not worthwhile.

What, then, should we do if we do not negotiate with a tyranny?

Win.

CHAPTER NINETEEN

MOST OFTEN REPORTED AND TAUGHT: (2011—CURRENT) ISOLATIONISM IS FINE ON THE LEFT AND NOW SUPPORTED BY MANY ON THE RIGHT

THE TRUTH:

IT IS AN INHUMANE AFFLICTION NO MATTER ITS FOLLOWERS

"Non-interventionism" has been and remains the acceptable way of isolationists advocating their philosophy because isolationists don't like being called isolationists. Regardless of their own terminology, such a philosophy is an inherent selfishness absent of every great religion's Golden Rule which has been expressed in one way and language after another: "Do unto others as you would have others do unto you." Instead, the term "non-interventionism" is an expression to do away with our traditional morality through most generations-past and generation-current. If our national interest means that our people and government should ignore far-away genocides and far-away despots, then our national interest is no longer admirable, nor is it still worthy of the respect the United States has gained and upheld throughout most of the 20th Century.

Such advocates quote from George Washington's Farewell Address of 1796, "Why quit our own, to stand upon foreign ground? Why, by interweaving our destiny with any part of Europe, entangle our peace and prosperity in the toils of European ambition, rivalship, interest, humor or caprice? 'Tis our true policy to steer clear of permanent alliances with any portion of the foreign world..."

Was George Washington right? Of course he was right for his times in that statement of 1797. The times dictated the correctness of what he said. The objective of the American Revolution, sustained all the way through the Nineteenth Century, was liberty for ourselves without diversions of cause. Such isolationism was not a profound decision but a logical one under the circumstances of nothing more complex than geography. Very large oceans left the nation isolated. But during the 20th Century our objective expanded because the role of the oceans diminished.

That is when U.S. objectives became both liberty at home and liberty beyond our shores where other people were at risk from tyrannies. As a result, the Twentieth Century is recognized throughout the world by friend and foe alike as the Century of the United States. Without us, it would have been known as the Century of Nazism or the Century of Communism, whichever of the two powers would have won the final battle, not that it would have made much difference since either way it would have been the Century of Slavery.

If we should go back to drawing the defensive line only at our own shores, then what will the current century be called? Will it be known as the Century of the Radical Islamic Jihadist Revolution or the Century of the People's Republic of China or the Century of a new Russian hegemony or the Century of the United Nations Organization or the Century of something beyond the horizon currently unborn?

Before World War II prominent isolationists were Charles Lindbergh, Father Charles Coughlin, Congressman Hamilton Fish, Congressman John Rank and Col. Robert McCormack, (publisher of the *Chicago Tribune*). During the Cold War there was the very prominent Republican Senator Robert Taft. Then, still within the Cold War, isolationism that used to be largely Republican became an instrument of Democrats in the McGovern Presidential Campaign of 1972 with the slogan, "Come Home, America." He lost 49 States. [The re-election of President Nixon won those states while Senator George McGovern won only Massachusetts and D.C.]

Currently, isolationists are in both major political tickets: Democrats as well as a new and large slice going back to Republicans. Most prominent is their isolationism not only against any U.S. intervention but also against U.S. intelligence agencies.

They fear their privacy is being taken away by the National Security Agency. There was a successful effort to make the public believe that the Congress was voting for liberty because members of the Congress said the choice was between liberty vs. security. No it wasn't. The real choice was giving up a key device of national security intelligence vs. unjustified fear of giving up some petty privacy, and even that was not under risk. It was a question of whether or not the National Security Agency (NSA) could retain metadata of phone numbers so as to have a record of what phone numbers—not conversations—but what U.S. phone numbers of terrorists had been used repeatedly: to or from Yemen or Syria or Iran or Nigeria or anywhere there were known members of al Qaeda or ISIS or Boko Haram or any other known terrorist group. There was no listening to phone calls unless approved by a Judge. The country was even told by some members of the Congress that the government was guilty of violating the Fourth Amendment's mandate that the government cannot conduct searches and seizures. Not true. The Fourth Amendment claims it would be a violation to conduct *unreasonable* searches or seizures. It says *unreasonable*. The Jihadist threat puts our survival at stake and a need for survival is reasonable. Our intelligence agency is not trying to find out about who is dating who. Whether or not you have been seeing Mary Ann on Wednesday nights is not of interest. Sorry. It just isn't that important.

Why is it that so many have no problem with that knowledge being held by AT&T or Verizon or Sprint as it has been, but they have a problem knowing the National Security Agency has those numbers? Strange because in all the years since the end of November, 2001 with the inception of a log of numbers that started this, not one person is known to have had his or her privacy violated. Not so incidentally, in 1979 the Supreme Court decided that no one needs a warrant for retaining phone call number records and that it is not a violation of privacy. But, as of midnight of November the 29th of 2015, the law prohibits the National Security Agency from keeping those logs of numbers. The NSA now has to ask the particular phone company with the whole procedure up to the phone companies involved and they could well take months.

There are also fears of some mainly young Americans about the internet and all the organizations that thrive on photos and personal information you can send them. If you don't want anyone to see, hear, or read through the newer technologies, don't use them for what you don't want others to see or hear or read. Why is that so difficult? After all, we have been without those technologies and social media to no one's tears for most of recorded time. Is it really worth risking the NSA not having information that could tell our government that some member of ISIS in Syria is regularly contacting the guy who is in your science class?

If we lose the war then the victorious leader will be an Ayatollah or an Imam or a Mullah or someone else that did not win a national election, and that person will mandate that American's privacy will be gone in totality as of Day Number One of the Jihad's victory, with unthinkable consequences if the new laws are not observed.

One Senator during the twelfth year of this Jihadist World War has publically proclaimed that "James Clapper lied!" [James Clapper was the Director of National Intelligence.] And then he added. "And Edward Snowden told the truth!" Of course James Clapper lied! What does anyone think those in intelligence do: tell the world the truth? And tell the truth in front of a publicly televised committee? James Clapper had already taken an oath never to reveal national security information. Edward Snowden also took an oath of security but he disregarded that oath and stole every detail that could be stolen and revealed all the classified information he could put on a digital hard drive and then made it all public throughout the world—and accepted refuge in Russia.

Yet to some in the Congress he is considered to be a hero; a whistleblower. All of this while the nation and much of the world was at war against Radical Islamist Jihadists. Former Director of the Central Intelligence Agency (CIA) and Former Director of the National Security Agency (NSA), Michael Hayden, described a whistleblower as someone who tells officials of the United States government information those officials should know but likely do not know. Snowden, instead, was telling the entire world; friend and foe alike.

The same Senator who placed blame on James Clapper and

praised Edward Snowden said he believes in "Peace through Commerce." (A little far-fetched that he stumbled on the solution for creating peace.)

We can win this war if we remember we are *in* one. We have the best all voluntary troops in the history of warfare and we have the best technology including the most advanced weaponry of any nation on earth—ever. A great misfortune is that we also have the most impatient people in the world. We live in the "Now Generation" grown-up. That is summarized in the true story told so often about the Afghanistan warlord talking to an American. The warlord looked at the American's left wrist and said, "You Americans have all the watches." The American looked down at his wrist and nodded. The warlord paused and then added, "And we have all the time."

Unfortunately many superb Libertarians have crossed the line into isolationism. It is so unfortunate because most Libertarians have tremendous merit in so many of their policies, particularly regarding domestic and economic leadership where they excel. But they don't seem to be done with those in their ranks that don't care if the oppressed live in freedom or slavery. That overreaches the thoughtfulness of Libertarianism into the arena of horror.

Most Americans might well be Libertarians if everyone in the world was good—or if all Libertarians drew a line between their own goodness and nonchalance in the acceptance of evil during their time on earth, as long as they don't have to watch it.

CHAPTER TWENTY

MOST OFTEN REPORTED AND TAUGHT: (Many Years Including Current) "THERE ARE TEN NATIONAL HOLIDAYS"

THE TRUTH:

THERE AREN'T ANY

The federal government designates holidays only for federal workers and for all those working in the District of Columbia since that entity is a federal district. They are called Federal Holidays and are not national or designated as being days-off for others. The States designate their own holidays and they, naturally, are called State Holidays. Even many cities have their own holidays. It has nothing to do with any other entity. But it does not mean there can't be State Holidays in which a State Legislature or Governor proclaims a State Holiday that can be the same date as a Federal Holiday or a different date and/or a different commemoration.

Most Federal Holidays have been adopted by all the States separately with some on different dates than others and some States call some holidays by different names than they have been named by other States.

The city of Vicksburg, Mississippi, surrendered to the Union on July 4, 1863 and didn't celebrate July the 4th for the next 82 years (until 1945) with that date finally recognized because so many from Vicksburg had been killed or missing in World War II.

Congress passed a holiday for federal workers and D.C. as a commemoration for Martin Luther King's birthday on the third Monday in every January and that was signed by President Reagan. Like most people, Reverend King was not born on the third Monday of every January but, rather in his case on January the 15th of 1929 which happened to be the third Tuesday of that year but nothing in the federal government is meant to be logical as a sole criterion.

Since 1971 what is known as the commemoration for George Washington's Birthday in the federal government and D.C. is now known as President's Day in some States commemorating any or all Presidents depending on the choice of the State. To briefly illustrate the difficulty that can arrive from all this, the students at public schools in California receive the day off from school to recognize President's Day while the mail does not get delivered to California residents and businesses on that day because the U.S. Postal Service is taking a Federal Holiday commemorating George Washington's birthday alone with nothing to do with any other President.

The birthday of Jefferson Davis, the President of the Confederacy has no federal celebration but is celebrated to this day (2015) in four southern states on his birthday of June the 3rd and celebrated on other dates in some other southern states.

Much of this particular mess was guaranteed when the Congress voted in favor of the 1971 Uniform Monday Holiday Act deciding that in addition to Labor Day that was already on a Monday, some additional Federal Holidays should be moved to Mondays—

giving more long weekends to federal workers and D.C. Prior to then, President Washington's birthday had been celebrated by federal workers and D.C. businesses and residents on his birthday of February the 22nd. In the new list of holidays President Washington's birthday received a commemoration—not on his birthday but on the third Monday of every February—and President Lincoln still couldn't make his name on the federal calendar; not even being given a crummy Monday.

CHAPTER TWENTY-ONE

MOST OFTEN REPORTED AND TAUGHT: (Current) "WORDS MEAN WHAT THEY SAY"

THE TRUTH: NOT IN GOVERNMENT

If you can't be told precisely what is meant by someone using a word with a questionable meaning, don't quickly nod to be agreeable:

When you hear the word "comprehensive" added to the title of an agreement, be it comprehensive immigration reform or a comprehensive Middle East Agreement or comprehensive anything, it means be careful. "Comprehensive" in diplomatic terms means every problem connected with the issue is addressed in this conclusive document, like it or not. All arguments have been decided and resolved in this one agreement.

"Targeted Tax Cuts" means that government will decide who

will be the winners and the losers in the distribution of taxpayer's funds.

The word "investment" is used instead of using the word "spending" or "taxation." What it means is that you will be charged for the investment since nothing can be invested without funds, and the federal government does not have funds earned on its own. Instead, it owes a tremendous debt. (Over 18 trillion dollars at this writing.)

Why is the word "big" used to describe a perceived evil? Why is there no "little oil" or "little tobacco" or "little insurance companies" or "little pharmacies"? Because it's hard to condemn anything with a pronoun like "little." "Big" works.

An "undocumented" immigrant means an illegal immigrant. But saying "undocumented" sounds like some immigrant mistakenly left his documents in his other pants.

The phrase, "Pro-Choice" is incomplete. Pro-choice of what? Pro-Choice of the school to which you want to send your child? Pro-Choice of a weapon for self-defense? Pro-Choice of joining or not joining a union? Maybe it's Pro-Choice of abortion but that is never said. The objective is not to use the word "abortion" because it puts too many horrible visuals in the minds of listeners.

The statement that "Roe v. Wade (1973) made abortion legal" is an annual inaccuracy that is made by many media every January the 22nd since 1973. The inaccuracy is that abortion was already legal in any State that wanted it before the decision of Roe v. Wade. The Supreme Court decision of Roe v. Wade, instead, made it illegal for a State to make its choice. Prior to January the 22nd of 1973 it was as legal as it is today in New York City, Washington, D.C., Washington State, Hawaii, and Alaska while 17 other States had their choices in various degrees of legality depending on circumstances as judged by voters of the State or State legislatures.

"Global Warming" sounded much too outrageous, particularly during cold winters, and so the phrase was changed to "Climate Change." This was much better since climate has been changing every three months or so (which used to be referred to as "seasons.") The imprecision of some weather-changing events made "The Coming Ice Age" the hysteria of the first Earth Day in 1970 and "Global Warming" the hysteria of the 30th Earth Day of 2000 and "Climate Change" the best yet because of so many thousands of years of frequency that have already passed, forecasting many years to come for the cause to receive funds.

It used to be that an "Opposition Researcher" was a noble political profession that helped candidates in researching the policy beliefs of those who were running against the candidate as well as their opponents preference in supporting and opposing candidates in previous elections. But more and more, near the end of the 20th Century that noble profession switched to the work of a private detective who would interview friends of the opposition; even childhood friends, to find out if they might know something that could sound like a vote-loser.

No longer are problems in government expressed as "problems" or "difficulties" or "troubles" or "a mess." Now all of those words have been deleted from government vocabularies in favor of saying those things are "challenges." That sounds much better and seems to have a greater chance of being overridden.

Many of those who run for office now preface their ideas with the phrase, "The American people want..." as though the candidate really knows. It's all a fraud while the candidate tells the audience what the candidate wants the people to endorse, likely not knowing or even considering what the American people want.

"Disproportionate" has often been used to criticize the reaction of the United States military or the militaries of U.S. Allies in response to attacks from an enemy. The complaint is that the response did not need to be that strong. But that doesn't take into consideration that a disproportionate response is vital to win. In contrast, a proportionate response guarantees either a loss or, at best, the battle will achieve a temporary stalemate until the enemy is able to win. We should always be disproportionate in battle and encourage our allies to do the same so as to achieve victory.

"Complicated" is the politician's best friend when the politician is questioned about a particular political subject that mystifies the politician who is being questioned. "To start off, we should all realize that we are talking about a very complicated subject with a lot of facets" is a passable answer for anything. The person questioning that politician should come back with, "We have time. Tell me all the complications and how you feel we should handle them." In truth, nothing in political life is complicated other than four subjects: the federal budget process, the rules governing the 1040 form of the Internal Revenue Service, the health care system, and U.S. policy toward China. And those things have been planned to be complicated so as to insure the public doesn't understand them—and certainly the politician doesn't understand them.

CHAPTER TWENTY-TWO

MOST OFTEN REPORTED AND TAUGHT:
(Many Years including Current)
"DEFENSE SPENDING IS TOO HIGH AND SHOULD BE CUT LIKE OTHER ELEMENTS OF THE U.S. BUDGET"

THE TRUTH:

NOT TOO HIGH IN THESE TIMES AND PERHAPS NOT IN ANY TIME

"Defense-spending" has been a repeated expression used by the major media. Defense is the only budget item that has a hyphen and the word "spending" attached to it. There is never a reference to "Food Stamp-spending" or "Housing and Urban Development-spending" or "Homeless-spending" or "Health-spending" or "Arts and Humanities-spending" or "Welfare-spending" or "Environmental Control-spending" or "Amtrak-spending," or "Social Security-spending" or "Corporation for Public Broadcasting-spending." The constant reference to "Defense-spending" has easily helped create the impression that it is the major cost of government. It is likely why an increased section of the public has demanded that as long as government's expenses must be lowered, defense must take its place along all other items in the budget.

Unlike any other budget item, a successful defense is based on the unknown. We can estimate how many interstate highways will be needed, how many social security payments have been promised, and how many national parks will be maintained. Defense is a guess. It is dependent on the decisions of many nations throughout the world beyond our own. If we guess too high on our budget for defense, we risk throwing away money that proved to be an unnecessary expenditure. If we guess too low, we risk throwing away the United States.

On September 1, 1993, Secretary of Defense Les Aspin announced the then-current trimmed-down military plan of the government. He explained that "We'll have a force based on tomorrow's requirements." It was as though tomorrow's requirements were known despite the absence of any U.S. Department of Prophecy that would have predicted the 9-11 of eight years forward and the years of Radical Islamist Jihadism beyond 9-11.

Most important of all is that unlike any other single budget item, the very survival of the United States can rest, and has rested, on defense. Currently budgeted for Fiscal Year 2016, while the United States is in a war against Radical Islamist Jihadists, President Obama has proposed a federal budget with 21% to be used for the nation's defense. For a nation at war, that is not high.

In the last full Fiscal Year of World War II; our defenses received 89½% of the federal budget leaving 10½% for everything else.

Complaints were few if any. It cost a lot but it didn't cost the existence of the country. We won.

[What is today called the Department of Defense was, in those days, called the Department of War. Fiscal Year '45 was planned by President Roosevelt and the 78th Congress. Fiscal Year '45 started on July the First of 1944 and ended on June the 30th of 1945.]

If sequestration goes through, (automatic budget cuts over a decade's time,) the U.S. Air Force will be reduced to its numbers prior to the time it was a separate military service; the U.S. Army and U.S. Marines will be reduced to their status prior to Pearl Harbor; and the U.S. Navy will be reduced to the status it had during the administration of Woodrow Wilson. President Obama, on November the 21st of 2011 warned the Congress to retain sequestration, saying: "Already some in Congress are trying to undo these automatic spending cuts. My message to them is simple. No! I will veto any effort to get rid of those automatic spending cuts to domestic and defense spending. There will be no easy off-ramps on this one."

Even without sequestration, by mid-2015 the U.S. Army had cut 40,000 troops, the U.S. Marines took a 10% cut in funds, the U.S. Navy had to take one Aircraft Carrier from the Persian Gulf and the U.S. Army received a 13.5% reduction.

The federal budget should never determine our defenses. Our defenses should determine the budget.

During the current World War only one nation, the United States so uncharacteristically has announced, "We will have no boots on the ground." It is beyond imagination for President Roosevelt to have made such a directive for the United States during World War II regarding his reaction to what was happening in Europe and Asia and North Africa. Would anyone who knows history have endorsed it? If he did say we would not have boots on the ground, I believe that the only people he would have pleased would have been our enemies. But now some Americans in both political parties applaud such a statement. Would any of those retain such a policy if someone they loved was being held by Radical Islamist Jihadists? If they can't say "yes" then they should endorse our "boots on the ground" as did the Greatest Generation.

There is the fact that the Constitution says that the Congress shall have power to declare war. But Congress cannot "wage"or "make" or "accomplish" it. Declaration of wars have been made by the Congress only five times in U.S. history, [the War of 1812, The Mexican-American War, the Spanish-American War, World War I and World War II,] but there have been some 240 U.S. foreign military engagements under the Constitutional authority of Presidents by holding the position of Commander in Chief. Allowing that power to be taken by the Congress, [as done by the 94th Congress] is exactly how we lost Vietnam after winning it previously under the authority of the President.

Counterpointing the past with the current and the future, our nation can do nothing of value for itself and nothing of value for the world if it doesn't survive. Decades back President Franklin Delano Roosevelt enlisted the support of the entire nation in attaining victory of the then-current world war. Without precedence, every American would have a role.

His State of the Union Address of January the 6th of 1942, thirty days after Pearl Harbor, is still significant by its masterful leadership, by the putting together of a knowledgeable list of the work ahead, and by making previously unheard requests of the people and then having those requests granted willingly and even fervently by the people. The following are excerpts from that Address:

"Victory requires the actual weapons of war and the means of transporting them to a dozen points of combat...This production of ours in the United States must be raised far above present levels, even though it will mean the dislocation of the lives and occupations of millions of our own people. We must raise our sights all along the production line. Let no man say it cannot be done. It must be done—and we have undertaken to do it.

"I have just sent a letter of directive to the appropriate departments and agencies of our Government, ordering that immediate steps be taken: First, to increase our production rate of airplanes so rapidly that in this year, 1942, we shall produce 60,000 planes, 10,000 more than the goal that we set a year and a half ago. This includes 45,000 combat planes [including] bombers, dive bombers, pursuit planes. The rate of increase will be maintained and continued so that next year, 1943, we shall produce 125,000 airplanes, including 100,000 combat planes. Second, to increase our production rate of tanks so rapidly that in this year, 1942, we shall produce 45,000 tanks; and to continue that increase so that next year, 1943, we shall produce 75,000 tanks. Third, to increase our production rate of anti-aircraft guns so rapidly that in this year, 1942, we shall produce 20,000 of them; and to continue that increase so that next year, 1943, we shall produce 35,000 anti-aircraft guns. And fourth, to increase our production rate of merchant ships so rapidly that in this year, 1942, we shall build 6,000,000 deadweight tons as compared with a 1941 completed production of 1,100,000. And finally, we shall continue that increase so that next year, 1943, we shall build 10,000,000 tons of shipping.

"Our task is hard—our task is unprecedented—and the time is short. We must strain every existing armament-producing facility to the utmost. We must convert every available plant and tool to war production. That goes all the way from the greatest plants to the smallest—from the huge automobile industry to the village machine shop.

"Production for war is based on men and women—the human hands and brains which collectively we call Labor. Our workers stand ready to work long hours; to turn out more in a day's work; to keep the wheels turning and the fires burning twenty-four hours a day, and seven days a week. They realize well that on the speed and efficiency of their work depend the lives of their sons and their brothers on the fighting fronts.

"Production for war is based on metals and raw materials—steel, copper, rubber, aluminum, zinc, tin. Greater and greater quantities of them will have to be diverted to war purposes. Civilian use of them will have to be cut further and still further—and, in many cases, completely eliminated.

"War costs money. So far, we have hardly even begun to pay for it. We have devoted only 15 percent of our national income to national defense. As will appear in my Budget Message tomorrow, our war program for the coming fiscal year will cost 56 billion dollars or, in other words, more than half of the estimated annual national income. That means taxes and bonds and bonds and taxes. It means cutting luxuries and other non-essentials. In a word, it means an 'all-out' war by individual effort and family effort in a united country.

"Only this all-out scale of production will hasten the ultimate all-out victory. Speed will count. Lost ground can always be regained—lost time never. Speed will save lives; speed will save this Nation which is in peril; speed will save our freedom and our civilization—and slowness has never been an American characteristic...

"We are fighting to cleanse the world of ancient evils, ancient ills. Our enemies are guided by brutal cynicism, by unholy contempt for the human race. We are inspired by a faith that goes back through all the years to the first chapter of the Book of Genesis: 'God created man in His own image...'

"We on our side are striving to be true to that divine heritage. We are fighting, as our fathers have fought, to uphold the doctrine that all men are equal in the sight of God. Those on the other side are striving to destroy this deep belief and to create a world in their own image—a world of tyranny and cruelty and serfdom. That is the conflict that day and night now pervades our lives. No compromise can end that conflict. There never has been—there never can be—successful compromise between good and evil. Only total victory can reward the champions of tolerance, and decency, and freedom, and faith."

Since World War II was won the United States has been the only nation with both the power and the will to fight for the liberty of strangers. Some nations have had the will but not the power. Some have had the power but not the will. The U.S. has had and used both for Berliners, Koreans, Vietnamese, Cambodians, Laotians, Kuwaitis, Afghans, Iraqis, Somalis, Bosnians, Kosovars, Grenadians, Haitians, Panamanians, others.

It could be, however, that in current times (2015) the United States government has neither the will nor the power and does not want either. Worse yet is that so many voters also want neither. If that comes about what would that mean?

It can be known what it would mean by closing eyes and ears

and mouth and humanity. But it isn't what used to be called freeing millions and millions and millions and millions of people from totalitarians and it isn't what used to be called "being an American."

No longer the role of the cavalry with a bugler in the lead.

No more hugs for Americans from those who live in endangered countries.

No more rescuing of others.

But maybe we can control the climate to stick around 72 degrees. Then we can go to the beach any time we want.

SUBJECTS OF CHAPTERS

01 The Length of Time of the U.S. Military in Afghanistan
02 Government "Shut-Downs"
03 Jurisdictions of the President and the Congress
04 Vietnam if JFK had Lived
05 Responsibility for Surrenders of Vietnam and Cambodia
06 Why Hong Kong was Given Back to China
07 A "One State" solution for China and Taiwan
08 A "Two State Solution" for Israel and a Palestinian State
09 The 1975 Church Committee and Consequences for Intelligence Agencies
10 National Security Sharing between the President and the Congress
11 The War Powers Act Constitutionality
12 President Nixon and his Presidency
13 The U.S. Government and the Rights Given in the Constitution
14 The Reading and Non-reading of Bills by Members of the Congress
15 Rights of the People in Peace and War
16 President Reagan on his Strategic Defense Initiative
17 President George W. Bush and Iraq
18 Negotiations with Foreign Powers
19 Isolationism
20 National Holidays
21 Words Used in Government
22 "Defense-Spending"

CPSIA information can be obtained at www.ICGtesting.com
Printed in the USA
LVOW07*0049070616

491460LV00002B/2/P

9 780825 308321